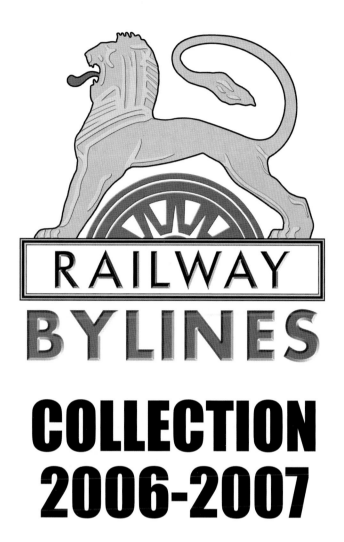

RAILWAY BYLINES

COLLECTION
2006-2007

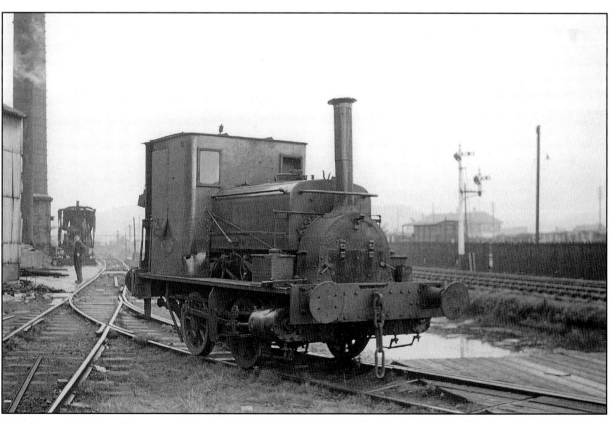

The former Wantage Tramway Manning Wardle 0-4-0T No.7 at Cordes Steelworks, Newport, on 25 February 1961. *Photograph: Peter Barnfield*

We made no fewer than sixteen visits to the Backworth railway system during the four-year period between April 1971 to April 1975. Backworth, as we knew it, was both in mining terms and in the extent of the internal railway system, a mere shadow of its former self. Not that we were aware of this at the time. To us, it was still a local shrine with a number of steam locomotives on various shifts, working hard for their keep each and every day.

Though not as extensive as the more famous coal railways of the north-east such as the Lambton Hetton & Joicey system, the NCB railway system centered on Backworth had many inter-connecting tendrils to surrounding collieries. However, it was the latter-day connection with Burradon and Weetslade in particular that was to endure until the end. More of this later.

The Pits

Mining had been undertaken in the vicinity of Backworth since the early 1700s but the industry did not get underway on a large scale until the early 1800s. Over the years the Backworth Coal Company and its successor, Backworth Collieries Ltd, operated several pits in the area, though not all were operational simultaneously. The principal ones were:

Backworth 'A': This, the first major pit at Backworth itself, was sunk in 1813 (just to put things in perspective that's two years before the Battle of Waterloo) and the first coal was shipped on 10 September 1818. It was later designated the 'A' pit. The date of its closure seems to have gone unrecorded, but is believed to have been in the early 1890s.

Backworth 'B': The second pit at Backworth opened in 1821 and was titled the 'B' pit. It was ½-mile north of the 'A' Pit. It closed in the 1890s.

West Cramlington Colliery: Opened in 1838, it was approximately three miles to the north of Backworth 'A'. The main line of the colliery tramway system was extended to serve it and in 1849 was further extended to join the York Newcastle & Berwick Railway (later NER). The pit was sold to the West Cramlington Coal Co in 1892 and the tramway serving it was subsequently lifted.

Backworth 'C': Situated about two miles north of Backworth, this pit was sunk alongside the tramway to West Cramlington in 1856 and effectively replaced the 'A' Pit for the drawing of coal. Although abandoned as long ago as 1895 the site was retained until the late 1970s for the tipping of 'stone' (colliery waste).

Fenwick Colliery: Situated to the east of the village of Earsdon, the first pit on this site – East Holywell Colliery (owned by the logically titled East Holywell Coal Co) – was begun in 1828. Fenwick Colliery was sunk here in 1860 and this name was adopted for the workings. Fenwick was served by a one-mile long branch line which was originally worked by a stationary engine. The colliery closed on 31 August 1973.

Bates Colliery: Originally known as East Holywell 'C' Pit (a name which it officially retained until the end), it was in the village of Holywell and was served by a one-mile extension of the railway beyond Fenwick Colliery. The date of its opening is uncertain. By NCB days the colliery was used only as a pumping and ventilation shaft for Fenwick Colliery but it nevertheless retained a rail connection to a coal depot until 1957, in which year the line beyond Fenwick was lifted.

Maude Pit: Sunk next to the site of Backworth 'A' Pit, it went into production in June 1872 and closed on 2 December 1960.

Algernon Pit: Originally a fairly small pit owned by the Shiremoor Coal Co, it was sunk in 1784 and closed in the 1830s. The Shiremoor company was taken over by the Backworth company in 1896 and, under the new owners, Algernon recommenced production in February 1898. It remained in operation until 19 February 1966.

Eccles Pit: In 1905/06 a new shaft was sunk some 200 yards north of the Maude Pit. This became known as the Eccles Pit after Richard Eccles, one of the Backworth company's directors, and commenced production in 1907. It was destined to become synonymous with Backworth. At 1,440 feet it was the deepest pit in the Northumberland Coalfield. By 1971 it was still employing 842 people, almost equally split between surface workers (424) and underground workers (418). It closed in

Just six weeks later – on 24 March 1970 – RSH 0-6-0STs Nos.44 and 47 were outside the shed. The loco coal wagons on the far right are on the road which went into the 'lean to' part of the shed. *Photograph: Ian S.Carr*

This 25-inch Ordnance Survey map of 1913 (reduced to approximately 17½in to the mile) helpfully identifies Eccles Pit and Maude Pit; it also acknowledges both as being 'Backworth Colliery'. If that sounds confusing, the article will explain. In later years – i.e. after this map was published – sidings were added in the fork of the lines near the level crossing (these sidings were on the site of the former Bell Engine), and *circa* 1970 the terraces of houses to the north of the colliery were demolished. *Crown Copyright*

were at the Eccles/Maude site.

It should be pointed out that the foregoing list of collieries refers only to those which were closely involved with the Backworth railway system. There were in fact several other collieries and associated brick-works which came and went during a period of 150 or so years, but they had disappeared before my time and are therefore beyond the remit of this article. It should also be pointed out that Blue Bell Disposal Point, which is shown on the accomanying map, is similarly beyond the remit of this article. The Disposal Point was operated by the Ministry of Fuel & Power and subsequently by the NCB's Opencast Executive and remained in use until 1959, but it had its own locomotives and was never worked as part of the Backworth system.

The railway

The Backworth Colliery Railway started life as a wooden waggonway in 1765 and extended for 3¾ miles from pits at Murton and Shiremoor to staithes on the River Tyne at Whitehill Point. The system closed *circa* 1810 but was later reopened – having been relaid with cast iron rails – on a diverted alignment to Backworth 'A' Pit. As new pits were sunk the railway system was extended accordingly. At its greatest extent, its northernmost extremity was the junction with the NER main line north of West Cramlington Colliery; this was some nine miles from the staithes on the Tyne. The system was originally worked by horses but in 1824 a rope haulage system, operated by stationary engines, was brought into use. Locomotive working seems to have been introduced in – or possibly before – 1861, but rope haulage remained in use on parts of the railway system until 1867. At the time the National Coal Board came into existence in 1947, the Backworth railway system served the four surviving collieries (Algernon, Eccles,

May 1980 and rail traffic ceased on 17 July 1980. By way of comparison, at the height of their life in 1950 the collieries of the Backworth system – Algernon, Eccles, Fenwick and Maude – employed between them a total of 2,905 people, of whom 1,502

A classic 'industrial steam shed' scene – inside the shed at Eccles colliery on 27 August 1974 were Austerities Nos.6, 48 (at the rear), the 'other' 48 (far right – only the bunker visible) and 49, and outside-cylindered RSH No.16. The door at the end of the right-hand road led to the workshop. *Photograph: Tom Heavyside*

Fenwick and Maude) and had no less than thirteen locomotives.

By the time I got to know the railway system in the 1970s it had been considerably truncated, a consequence of pit closures. It now served just two collieries: Fenwick and Eccles. A very recent loss had been that of the southern section of the line to Whitehill Point Staithes. Traffic to the staithes had ceased on 24 August 1969 and the line was later lifted south of a spot known as West Allotment Siding, a little to the south of the point where it crossed what is now the A186 road near Backworth station. The surviving stub to West Allotment subsequently served as a headshunt.

Following the closure of the line to the staithes, most of the rail-borne coal from Fenwick and Eccles collieries was exchanged with BR at newly-laid sidings at Earsdon Junction, where the NCB's Fenwick Pit line crossed BR's Blyth & Tyne line. However, that arrangement was fairly short-lived as, following the partial collapse of the washery at Eccles Colliery in 1970, the coal was taken on to Weetslade Colliery for washing and was collected from there by BR locomotives.

Eccles Colliery and yard
When describing the walk from Backworth station to the NCB depot, mention was made of the level crossing at Station Road. Immediately to the north of this crossing the line diverged; one limb struck

determinedly northwards to the heart of the system at Eccles Colliery, while the other curved through some 90 degrees to strike out eastwards to the Fenwick Pit. In the 'V' between the diverging lines was a cylindrical water tank atop brick pillars. Part way around the curve of the Fenwick Pit line was a series of coal stocking sidings (the Bell Sidings, named after the Bell Engine – the stationary engine – which was once on the site); these sidings usually gave us our first sight of the resident locomotives, as invariably one was merrily shunting here.

The line heading for Eccles Colliery itself almost immediately spread into a series of holding loops, which included the weighbridge road on the western extremity. One road had a simple water crane, where it seemed that all locos could satisfy their liquid requirements. This area was also festooned with street-like concrete lamp-posts, overhead electricity cable pylons and telegraph wires. The series of holding loops disappeared into the Eccles Colliery screens. On the eastern side of the loops and opposite the screens was the locomotive shed. One line – the running line – plied a direct but constricted route between the screen roads and the wall of the engine shed. To the north of the screens the loop lines gathered themselves back together and rejoined the running line, which continued its bee-line northwards to cross Church Street at the northern end of the colliery yard. The crossing itself was

known as the School Crossing because of the school on its north-east side.

The Fenwick Pit line
The line from Eccles Yard to Fenwick Pit was about one mile in length and on a fairly steep grade up from Fenwick to Eccles. This necessitated the use of two locos to lift a rake of loaded coal wagons. The usual practice was to have one engine at the front and one at the rear. A feature of the line from Fenwick Pit was the 90-degree flat crossing it made with BR's Blyth & Tyne line. On the south-east side of this crossing was a spur off the NCB line making a connection with the BR line to the south. In the triangle thus formed was BR's Earsdon signal box which controlled signals on the NCB line guarding the flat crossing. Having crossed over the BR metals, trains from Fenwick Pit continued to work hard as they came into the south-eastern environs of Eccles Yard. Near the Bell coal stocking sidings the trains passed under a gantry affair that looked to me as if it were a defunct watering facility. The trains then had to veer to the south, cross the B1322, and enter the headshunt which had been created from the truncated staithes line. The trains could then reverse back across the road and into Eccles Colliery yard.

The 'Stone Tippler' line
Beyond School Crossing at the north end of Eccles Colliery yard, the running line

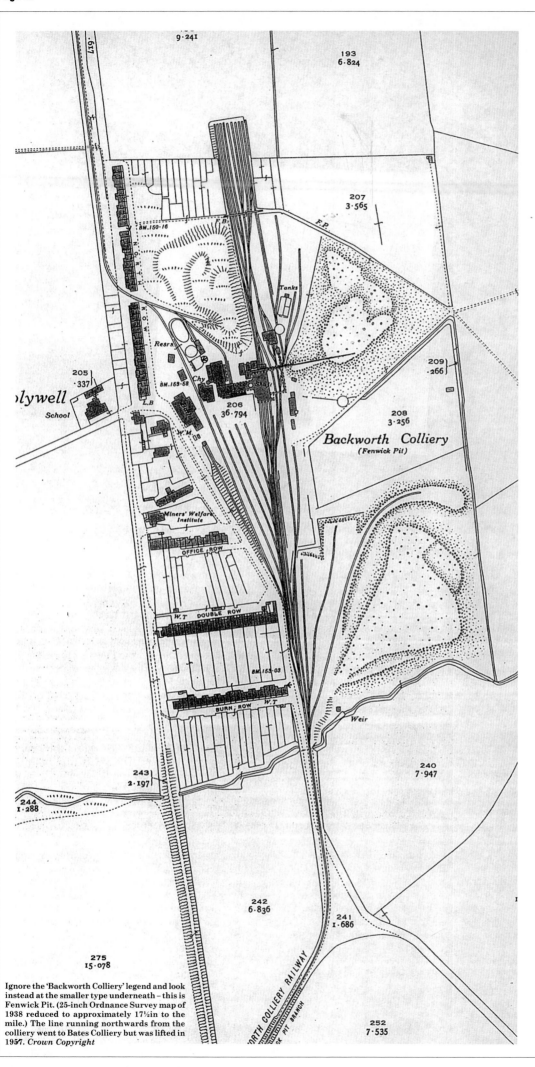

Ignore the 'Backworth Colliery' legend and look instead at the smaller type underneath – this is Fenwick Pit. (25-inch Ordnance Survey map of 1938 reduced to approximately 17½in to the mile.) The line running northwards from the colliery went to Bates Colliery but was lifted in 1957. *Crown Copyright*

continued, now on a falling grade, and passed to the east of the site of the old Backworth 'B' Colliery. In the early 1970s this was given visual substance by means of a few short overgrown sidings, with some derelict looking NCB hopper wagons adjacent to a strangely decorative concrete and brick edifice with a crenellated top. Though I knew not at the time, this was in fact the remains of an old washery, known locally as the 'Dolly Washer', which had been built on the site of the old 'B' pit. After the closure of the 'Dolly Washer' in 1940 the building had been given an extended lease of life as a wagon paint shop, even as late as 1972. The railway continued northwards past the 'Dolly Washer' and headed straight down what had at one time been a rope-worked incline for about half a mile before being crossed at almost right-angles. The crossing line came from Burradon Colliery (approximately 1¾ miles to the west) and went to exchange sidings with the Blyth and Tyne Railway. The line to Burradon Colliery was of particular interest, as it had been built in 1911/12 by the NER. At least one of the original NER signals remained *in situ*, even in the 1970s when the line had long since been part of the NCB.

To the north of Eccles colliery our line continued to the site of the old Backworth 'C' Pit which had been abandoned in 1895. The line had nevertheless been retained and was used to dump stone (colliery waste), hence its title of the 'Stone Tippler'. On our third visit on 17 August 1971 we walked down to the stone tippler and met up with locomotive No.47. The crew was kind enough to give us a ride back up to Eccles Yard. The ride itself was of course memorable, particularly for the noise in the cab and the buffeting received during the all-out effort made by the loco as it tackled the incline. There

Austerity No.54 takes water at Eccles Colliery on 19 August 1969. This loco had been transferred from Ashington Shed just three months earlier but was to have only a short life on the Backworth system as it was scrapped in October 1969 – just two months after this picture was taken. In the distance is the level crossing over the B1322 and the associated cabin. On the left, the water tank is standing on the site of the Bell Engine, the stationary engine which worked the Fenwick Colliery branch. *Photograph: Ian S.Carr*

RSH 0-6-0T No.29 was one of only two side tank locos on the Backworth system in the 1960s and 1970s. Being the very first Backworth loco the author ever witnessed in full flight, it was a particular favourite. Here we see it taking water at Eccles Colliery on 19 August 1969. *Photograph: Ian S.Carr*

Backworth Collieries Ltd's Whitehill Point staithes and surrounds, 25-inch Ordnance Survey map of 1938 reduced to approximately 17½in to the mile. *Crown Copyright*

We are looking towards the south end of Eccles Colliery yard on 19 August 1969. The now-preserved Austerity No.6 shunts while another now-preserved Austerity, No.48, takes water. Both locos are carrying a shunter's pole on the brackets just below the bunker. *Photograph: Ian S.Carr*

was also that sense of wanting to be in two places at the same time: on the footplate, but also at the lineside to photograph the vociferous spectacle. With the grade easing, we negotiated School Crossing and stormed through the chicane created by the screens and loco shed before finally halting alongside the weighbridge.

The Burradon connection

Strangely enough, it wasn't until as late as 1951 that a connection was laid at the point where the Backworth and Burradon lines crossed at Fisher Lane, a little to the north of Eccles. This connection, in the south-west corner of the crossing, gave direct access between Eccles Colliery and Burradon and Weetslade collieries. Initially, despite the forging of a conduit between the two systems, they continued to operate essentially independently for a while but, as the years passed, the connection played an increasingly important role in the survival of the Backworth railway system. Some coal was brought from Burradon to the washery at Eccles and some colliery waste was also brought down to be tipped at the site of the old Backworth 'C' Pit. The situation with regard to washing coal was reversed in 1970 as a result of the partial collapse of the washery at Eccles. After this, all coal from Eccles was taken up the Burradon line and onwards to Weetslade Washery, one mile further east. A coal preparation

plant had been developed at Weetslade in the 1960s, and Weetslade Colliery itself had closed in 1966, but the traffic from Eccles to Weetslade continued until 1977. (See Tom Heavyside's article *The Weetslade Run* in the April 2001 edition of *Bylines*, Vol.6 No.5.)

Locomotive facilities

The engine shed at Eccles Colliery was a soot-encrusted two-road stone-built structure with a wooden lean-to extension with a single track on the right. Whenever we visited, the large doors to the main shed were invariably open but those of the lean-to were closed. There were two exception to this rule: our visits on Wednesday 26 July 1972 and Tuesday 2 January 1973. On these two occasions there was nothing working and the shed doors were firmly closed. The first date was on the occasion of a miners' strike, in sympathy with 50 dockers who had been jailed in Pentonville prison; the second was obviously a continuation of the New Year's Day celebrations.

At the front and on the east side of the shed was a rather unique coaling facility. It took the form of a conveyor belt which ran parallel to and between the rails from ground level, behind the siding, to an elevated hopper under which the locomotive bunker was positioned for receiving the coal. As for the shed building itself, on entering it one was plunged into

a cave-like gloom, the windows on the west side having long been rendered opaque with accumulations of grime. The dimpled stone floor was cold, with oily pools of water in all of its many surface depressions. The depths of the building were dimly lit by orange sodium lights. On the east side, archways gave access to the line covered by the lean-to. I never saw this line used by the colliery locomotives, but it eventually became a haven for industrial locomotives destined for preservation (see table). At the rear of the shed one of the lines continued through a doored opening into 'The Works'. This area housed the workshop and locomotive staff mess room. The workshop was indeed a scene of steady maintenance work throughout our visits; among the locomotives we noted 'in works' were:

13 May 1971: No.48* (Hunslet 2864)
17 August 1971: No.6 (Bagnall 2749)
21 August 1973: No.48* (Hunslet 3172)
24 October 1973: D9535 (ex-BR diesel)
25 April 1974: No.6 (Bagnall 2749)
9 April 1975: No.48* (Hunslet 3172)
(* The reference to two different 'No.48s' is not a mistake. The second one, Hunslet 3172, arrived at Backworth late in the day, having been transferred from Shilbottle Colliery, and the NCB clearly considered it superfluous to renumber it.)

The sight of D9535 in the shops on 24 October 1973 took us by surprise. This loco was one of BR's Swindon-built Paxman-

STEAM LOCOS BASED AT BACKWORTH (NCB) SHED, 1960 onwards (listed in order of acquisition)

Makers abbreviated thus: HC – Hudswell Clarke; **HE** – Hunslet Engine Co; **HL** – Hawthorn Leslie; **MW** – Manning Wardle; **RS** – Robert Stephenson; **RSH** – Robert Stephenson & Hawthorns; **RWH** – R.W.Hawthorn; **SS** – Sharp Stewart; **WB** – W.G.Bagnall

* Numbers: In 1951 the NCB introduced a renumbering scheme; it is those numbers which are shown in the first column. In September 1964 a new Area numbering system was introduced; these are the numbers shown in the second column.

¶ Details of acquisition and disposal shown in *italics* denotes that the loco was not at Backworth continuously between the dates shown (details at foot of table)

(P) Loco preserved (details below)

NCB numbers * First *	1964 *	Type	Maker; W/No.	Built	Wheel diameter	Cylinders	To Backworth shed	Disposal ¶
4	-	0-6-0ST	RS 2232	1875	4' 0"	14¾" x 22" (i)	12.1889	11.1960 Scrapped
1	-	0-6-0ST	RWH 1664	1876	4' 0"	15" x 22" (i)	1.1911	1.1961 Scrapped
16	16	0-6-0ST	HL 2671	1906	4' 1"	17" x 26" (o)	1906	c.10.1966 Scrapped
23	-	0-4-0ST	MW 1999	1921	2' 9¾"	10" x 16" (o)	1.1932	c.10.1961 to Bardon Mill Colliery c.10.1961
11	11	0-6-0ST	HC 555	1900	4' 0"	16" x 24" (i)	2.1934	11.1967 to Severn Valley Railway (P)
33	33	0-6-0ST	RSH 7177	1944	4' 3"	18" x 26" (i)	12.1944	9.1968 Scrapped
39	39	0-6-0T	HC 1824	1949	3' 9"	17" x 24" (i)	ex-Weetslade Colliery (date unknown)	10.1969 Scrapped
44	44	0-6-0ST	RSH 7760	1953	3' 10"	17" x 24" (o)	New	*3.1975 to Burradon for storage; later to Tanfield Railway* ¶ (P)
47	47	0-6-0ST	RSH 7849	1955	3' 10"	17" x 24" (o)	New	12.1971 to Whittle Colliery (P)
10	-	0-6-0PT	SS 4595	1900	4' 4"	17½" x 26" (i)	11.1955 ex-Rising Sun Colliery, Wallsend	1.1963 Scrapped
48	48	0-6-0ST	HE 2864	1943	4' 3"	18" x 26" (i)	12.1959 ex-Bluebell Disposal Point	6.1976 to Strathspey Railway (P)
49	49	0-6-0ST	RSH 7098	1943	4' 3"	18" x 26" (i)	*12.1959 ex-Bluebell Disposal Point*	*1.1976 to Burradon Sheds* ¶ (P)
24	24	0-6-0ST	HC 1489	1922	4' 0"	15" x 22" (o)	c.5.1960 ex-Weetslade Colliery	12.1967 Scrapped
10	7	0-6-0ST	HL 2835	1910	3' 10"	16" x 24" (o)	12.1960 ex-Seaton Delaval	8.1965 Scrapped
71497	3	0-6-0ST	HC 1774	1944	4' 3"	18" x 26" (i)	6.1961 ex-Pilsley Disposal Point, Derbyshire	11.1969 Scrapped
75061	9	0-6-0ST	RSH 7097	1943	4' 3"	18" x 26" (i)	*6.1961 ex-Newbattle Disposal Point, Midlothian*	6.1976 to Strathspey Railway (P) ¶
71512	4	0-6-0ST	RSH 7166	1944	4' 3"	18" x 26" (i)	*6.1961 ex-Newbattle Disposal Point, Midlothian*	8.1967 to Netherton Colliery ¶
75161	6	0-6-0ST	WB 2749	1944	4' 3"	18" x 26" (i)	7.1961 ex-West Hallam Disposal Point, Derbyshire	5.1977 to Bowes Railway (P)
38	56	0-6-0ST	RSH 7602	1949	4' 0"	18" x 24" (o)	1964 ex-Burradon Sheds	c.10.1966 to Burradon Sheds
49	49	0-6-0ST	WB 2750	1944	4' 3"	18" x 26" (i)	8.1967 ex-Ashington Sheds	10.1969 Scrapped
44	60	0-6-0ST	RSH 7812	1954	4' 0"	18" x 24" (o)	11.1967 ex-Burradon Sheds	8.1970 Scrapped
B17	15	0-6-0ST	RSH 7748	1953	4' 0"	18" x 24" (o)	7.1968 ex-Cambois Colliery	Boiler to No.60 2.1969; remains scrapped c.8.1969
35	35 CLIVE	0-6-0ST	RSH 7299	1946	3' 10"	17" x 24" (o)	2.1969 ex-Burradon Sheds	8.1969 to Burradon Sheds
54	54	0-6-0ST	HE 2866	1943	4' 3"	18" x 26" (i)	5.1969 ex-Ashington Shed	10.1969 Scrapped
29	29	0-6-0T	RSH 7607	1950	4' 6"	18" x 26" (o)	6.1969 ex-Ashington Shed	9.1972 Scrapped
62	16	0-6-0ST	RSH 7944	1957	4' 0"	18" x 24" (o)	*10.1971 ex-Bedlington Colliery*	*1.1976 to Burradon Sheds* ¶ (P)
48	48	0-6-0ST	HE 3172	1944	4' 3"	18" x 26" (i)	3.1973 ex-Shilbottle Colliery	1.1976 to Burradon Sheds

¶ Locos which left Backworth and subsequently returned:
44 – to Burradon Sheds 5.1973; returned to Backworth 10.1974
49 – to Burradon Sheds 1.1973; returned to Backworth 11.1973
3 – to North Walbottle Colliery 9.1963; returned to Backworth 1.1968
9 – to North Walbottle Colliery 7.1961; returned to Backworth 12.1971
4 – to Seaton Delaval Sheds 9.1962; returned to Backworth 7.1963
16 – to Burradon Sheds 9.1973; returned to Backworth 9.1974

Preserved locomotives
11 (Hudswell Clarke 0-6-0ST 555/1900): went to the Severn Valley Railway 11.1967. It is still there, awaiting restoration as GWR No.813.
44 (RSH 0-6-0ST 7760/1953): ceased work at Backworth by 3.1975 and transferred to Burradon sheds; acquired by the Tanfield Railway and moved back to Eccles shed for storage 2.1976. Moved to the Tanfield Railway 6.1980. It is still there, awaiting restoration.
48 (Hunslet 0-6-0ST 2864/1943): went to the Strathspey Railway; as far as we are aware it is still there.
9 (RSH 0-6-0ST 7097/1943): went to the Strathspey Railway; restoration work has recently started.
6 (Bagnall 0-6-0ST 2749/1944): went to the Bowes Railway 5.1977 but moved to the Caledonian Railway, Brechin, 8.1979. Was in regular use there until 1998 but is now out of use.
16 (RSH 0-6-0ST 7944/1957): ceased work at Burradon Sheds 3.1976 and moved to Eccles Colliery for storage 2.1977. Moved to the Tanfield Railway 6.1980; it is still there, awaiting restoration.
47 (RSH 0-6-0ST 7849/1955): ceased work at Whittle Colliery, 9.1973 and went to the North York Moors Railway. Later went to the Rother Valley Railway then to Peak Rail. Moved to the Lincolnshire Wolds Railway near Louth in April 1993; it is still there and is currently under restoration.
49 (RSH 0-6-0ST 7098/1943): ceased work at Burradon Sheds 3.1976 and moved to Eccles Colliery for storage 2.1977. Moved to the Tanfield Railway 6.1980; it is still there and is operational.

The north end of Eccles Colliery, photographed on 28 August 1974. The screens are on the right. Bagnall Austerity No.6 is hard at work on the running line. *Photograph: Tom Heavyside*

engined diesel hydraulics, a total of nineteen of which had been purchased by the NCB between 1967 and 1970, principally for use at Ashington Colliery. We feared that its presence at Eccles 'shops might be an indication that the Backworth loco fleet was about to succumb to dieselisation, but our enquiries revealed that it was only in for a repaint – it had a grey undercoat and was waiting to receive its dark blue NCB livery. Although diesels had taken over at most of the collieries in the area (by 1974 only three collieries in the north-east still had regular steam working), it was January 1976 before the Backworth system gained its first resident diesel.

As an aside, I remember the first time that we saw these former BR locos in the North-east was on Sunday 23 November 1969 when, to our great surprise, we found D9500 and D9517 languishing at the side of Gateshead shed *en route* to Ashington. Other examples had arrived as early as December the previous year. Later, we saw D9535 – the loco we had found being repainted at Eccles shed – at Burradon on 5 April 1972 (it was still in BR livery) and again on 2 January 1973.

.......ooooo000ooooo..........

The usual livery for the Backworth locos was the elegant Northumberland Area dark blue, with yellow shaded red lettering and red coupling rods. However, there were exceptions to this. In particular, RSH 0-6-0ST No.16 wore its black livery with off-white lining and off-white shaded lettering throughout the period of observations by the author, right up until April 1975. The former Shilbottle 'Austerity', No.48, arrived in black livery, which it retained until at least 25 April 1974; contemporary notes state that it was in dark blue livery on subsequent visits of 30 December 1974 and 9 April 1975, but can any reader confirm this apparent late repaint? Another exception was No.44 which wore a light blue livery. Probably the most resplendent of the stud was No.49, with its attractive livery of green with cream lining, cream lettering and red rods, now immortalized by Hornby in an 00 scale model.

In general, the locomotives were kept in quite clean condition; my recollections are of Nos.9 and 49 being particularly so. On 23 December 1971 I noted a very clean No.6 standing outside the front of the shed and a similarly clean No.9 inside the shed. Indeed, No.6 was so clean that one could read the silhouette of its original MoS number (75161) on the rear of the bunker. In winter time the locomotives sported improvised wooden shutters covering the cab side openings, a rather necessary protection against the harsh Northumberland weather.

Aesthetically complementing the dark blue locomotives, the majority of the wagon fleet was painted bright red. There were a variety of hopper designs. To my recollection the most prevalent were the (ex-Burradon) wooden hoppers which had 9-plank sloping sides and flat ends, bearing a strong family resemblance to North Eastern Railway wooden hoppers. There were similar wooden hoppers that were straight-sided with an inward bevel at the bottom and with open ends. The ubiquitous steel hoppers of 16-ton and 21-ton capacity were present at this time, as well as several simple straight-sided open wagons. There were also some special duty wagons, such as the tool van which was invariably parked on the line leading into the lean-to shed.

Personal sightings

The notes I took during my various visits to the Backworth system reveal the state of play with certain locomotives. For example:

9 – seen on shed but out of steam on 23 December 1971; this was shortly after its return to Backworth from Burradon.

29 – last seen stored in the shed on 2 March 1972; subsequently removed by road for scrapping.

44 and 49 – both seen on shed but out of use on 25 April 1974; neither was seen working again.

RSH 0-6-0ST No.60 eases a lengthy train of loaded wagons from Fenwick Colliery towards the junction with the NCB 'main line' near Eccles Colliery. In the distance another RSH 0-6-0ST (No.47) is seen dropping off the rear of the train, having banked it up the incline. No.47 has just cleared the point where the NCB line crossed BR's Blyth & Tyne on the level next to Earsdon signal box. The date is August 1970. *Photograph: J.W.Armstrong Trust*

A typical view of the north end of Eccles Colliery with Austerities Nos.6 and 48 on duty. The date is 28 August 1974. *Photograph: Tom Heavyside*

Austerity No.6 shunts at Eccles on 27 August 1974. In the distance is an ex-BR 'Paxman' (Class 14) which has worked in from Burradon Colliery. By this time the Paxmans were looking after much of the traffic between Eccles and Burradon. *Photograph: Tom Heavyside*

One of the visual delights of the Backworth system was the working of trains over the level crossing with the B1322 at the south end of Eccles Colliery. The crossing being ungated, trains had to be flagged across. This is Austerity No.6 crossing on 27 August 1974. *Photograph: Tom Heavyside*

No.6 is now propelling its train back towards Eccles yard. It is unlikely that the train had actually cleared the crossing during the manoeuvre shown in this and the previous photograph, so the motorists would have had to wait patiently during the whole procedure. The building on the left is the gatekeeper's cabin. *Photograph: Tom Heavyside*

The GWR shed alongside Malvern Road station in Cheltenham had had 'parent' status until the mid-1930s but then became a sub-shed of Gloucester (Horton Road). It nevertheless continued to be regarded as a bit of a special case as it was afforded its own allocation until the 1950s. This picture was taken on 10 September 1961. The pair of Prairies would no doubt have been involved with the working of the delightful 'cross-Cotswold' line to Kingham.

The modeller's dream – the superb little shed at St.Ives, photographed in September 1960. A sub of Penzance, its broad gauge origins are betrayed by the (standard gauge) track being offset to the left of centre. The shed's usual occupant was a 45XX Prairie – the versions with larger tanks were prohibited from the St.Ives branch. The shed closed in September 1961 following the dieselisation of the branch passenger workings.

THE WESTWARD TELEVISION TRAIN
by Jeffery Grayer

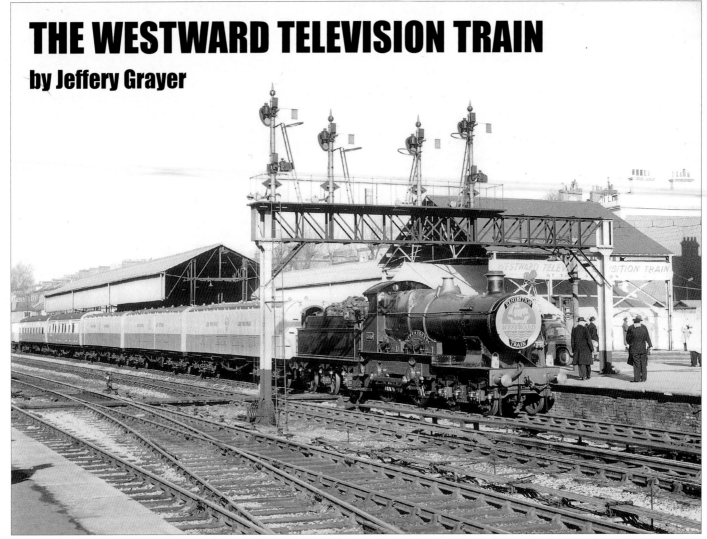

The Westward Television Exhibition Train stands at Kensington Olympia. As noted in the text the train spent three days at Olympia before setting out on its grand tour of the West Country. *City of Truro* needs no introduction, but it should nevertheless be noted that the Westward TV train tour was its very last duty before it became a static exhibit at Swindon Museum. Fortunately, though, the famous loco returned to action in 1984. *Photograph: Paul Chancellor Collection*

Exhibition Trains were used successfully for many years to advertise various products and services and, when the ITV network finally reached the West Country in 1961, an exhibition train extolling the virtues of the new service toured the principal towns served by the new television station. Even more imaginative – at least, from the railway enthusiast's point of view – was the ploy of using restored GWR legend *City of Truro* as the main motive power.

Although the first two regional ITV stations had opened in 1955 to serve London and the Midlands, it was to take a further six years before the independent network reached the South West. Some twelve franchise bidders entered the ring, but this was whittled down to just five and the eventual winner was Westward Television. Westward had hoped to get the transmitters operational by the beginning of 1961 but, in the event, broadcasting from their new studios in Plymouth was not possible until the end of April. In spite of the delays the flamboyant chairman of the fledgling company, Peter Cadbury, arranged to hire an exhibition train from BR to tour the major towns and cities of the new ITV region early in the New Year.

The choice of motive power was the famous ex-GWR 4-4-0 3440 *City of Truro*, which hauled the train for most – but not all – of its six-week tour of the West

Country. Although the use of *City of Truro* might have been inspired, the effect was dulled by a rather large circular headboard bearing the legend 'Westward Exhibition Train' obscuring most of the loco's smokebox door. The headboard, which was uncomfortably reminiscent of the 'Lyons Maid Zoom' monstrosity which would adorn the front of *Flying Scotsman* in 1964, did little for the splendid machine's front-end aesthetics. The exhibition itself was inaugurated at Kensington Olympia on 9 February 1961; it was opened by Sir Bernard Waley-Cohen, the Lord Mayor of London, who was actually a Westcountryman with a country seat at Simonsbath on Exmoor. He was presented with a television set, tuned to the appropriate channel, and a Westward Television tie with the station's galleon logo. In accepting the TV set the Lord Mayor said that he was '...*one of those rather old-fashioned people who've been*

rather slow in owning a television set and therefore it will be a terrific thing to have one of my own.' Other notable guests at the send-off were the Chairman of Cornwall County Council, the MP for Tavistock and the Mayor of Kensington, also a Westcountryman.

The exhibition train remained at Olympia until 11 February when it left for the South West.

The train

The train, which weighed in at 400 tons and was 435 feet in length, was painted strikingly in the television station's house colours of blue, white and yellow. The rake consisted of three Siphon Gs, two carriages, a generator van and a brake van. One coach had been converted by a specialist firm into a fully operational television studio which housed Videcon cameras, projectors, monitors, telecine and all the other 'magic boxes' that brought TV programmes to the home. The other coach was converted to a cinema and reception lounge for showing programme formats and entertaining both the public and potential advertisers. This contained the latest Bell & Howell model 640 16mm magnetic-optical sound projector and a refreshment bar. The cinema coach had forty seats – described as 'comfortable armchairs' – and showed extracts from TV

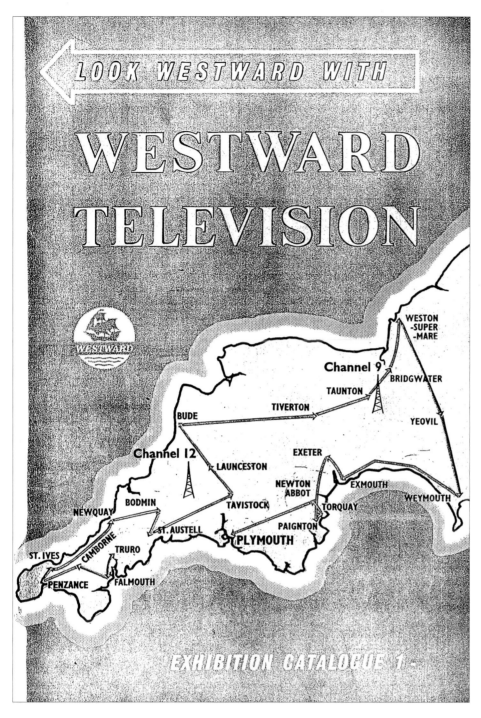

LOOK WESTWARD WITH

WESTWARD TELEVISION

EXHIBITION CATALOGUE 1

no longer served by the national network today. Considerable organisational and logistical work had gone into planning the tour with over 45 BR stations in the TV franchise area being visited in advance to check on platform lengths, car parking facilities, toilet arrangements, hotel accommodation, access to the train for the public, advertising sites etc. It is intriguing to speculate which towns the tour might have been expected to visit but for various operational reasons did not; it certainly appears that North Devon was somewhat under-represented and one might have thought that Barnstaple or Bideford would have been potential locations. Clarks Shoes, who were based in Street, had a display of their products on board so perhaps they quietly hoped that a visit to S&D territory at nearby Glastonbury & Street station on the Highbridge branch might also have been on the cards. However, this was not to be and the Mayor of Glastonbury had to be content with attending the Taunton event. W.D.& H.O.Wills displayed their tobacco wares, notably the 'Bristol' brand of cigarettes, but perhaps a visit to Bristol, even though the signal could be received there, was not considered politic situated as it was in the heart of territory served by the neighbouring franchisee, TWW (Television Wales & The West).

Where there was more than one station in a particular location, the one nearest the town centre was usually chosen as being the most likely to attract the public so, for example, in Tavistock the ex-GWR station (Tavistock South) was used and in Bodmin the ex-LSWR station (North) played host to the train. Similarly in Yeovil the centrally placed Town station and in Exeter the much more convenient Central station were used. At Weston-super-Mare the train used Locking Road Excursion station instead of the main station – this, however, was not to do with location (Locking Road was adjacent to the main station) but to avoid occupying precious space at the main station.

Perhaps the most picturesque location visited was St.Ives where by all accounts '...the train staff were delighted with the beautiful view of the harbour and beaches afforded from the train... a TV camera was soon in action taking views of the town from the train windows and these were shown "live" on the CCTV receivers accompanied by the cries of seabirds picked up on sound recording instruments.' This was no doubt a welcome change for the train's personnel after being parked in some siding in the middle of town.

More than 400,000 invitation tickets were distributed throughout the region to TV dealers, newsagents, hotels, the police, works canteens etc, and, for reasons that we have not been able to discover, also to the Women's Royal Voluntary Service. The usual procedure was to have a reception for the trade in the morning followed later in the day by public viewing. *City of Truro* was made available for inspection, steps being thoughtfully provided to allow access to the cab; this was no doubt much more attractive to certain members of the public than the exhibition itself.

The tour organisers paid tribute to BR

shows booked for the new station; these included 'Maverick', 'Wyatt Earp' and 'African Patrol', the showings being preceded by a short tele-recorded speech by Peter Cadbury. Other TV screens, of which there were 75 throughout the train, whetted the public's appetite by showing excerpts from ITV's big crowd pullers of the time: 'Emergency Ward 10', 'Bonanza', '77 Sunset Strip' and 'Saturday Night at the London Palladium'. The generator van housed a 60 k.v.a. diesel generator to power the cameras, TV sets, lighting and heating throughout the train and burned some 50 gallons of fuel daily.

The Siphon Gs were re-clad both internally and externally and exhibitors' stands were constructed which could be rented by local radio and television dealers wishing to sell new receivers, black and white of course in those days, to the general public. Although most television sets made in the preceding five years could receive the new transmission, dealers explained the conversion necessary, apparently

involving a small coil costing 7/6d, which allowed older sets to receive the new station and they even elaborated upon the direction in which to point aerials! There was a museum section in one of the coaches which displayed early receivers together with one of Marconi's original notebooks. The reporter for the *Bridgwater Mercury* explained to his readers that the train was '...the work of over 100 technicians, artists, designers, carpenters and electricians.' Other local journalists could not resist statistics: '...the materials used in the train's conversion included 13,000 feet of timber, 700 sheets of hardboard, 6 cwt of nails/panel pins, 75 gallons of paint, 1¼ miles of power cable linking over 360 lighting and power points, and 250 yards of carpet.'

On tour
The train visited 23 locations throughout the new franchise area. This involved journeys on main lines and branch lines and included five destinations which are

WESTWARD TELEVISION EXHIBITION TRAIN

At the following stations the historic Locomotive "City of Truro" will also be on display

TRURO   FALMOUTH
CAMBORNE   PENZANCE
NEWQUAY   ST. AUSTELL
TIVERTON   TAUNTON
BRIDGWATER   WESTON-SUPER-MARE
EXETER (CENTRAL)   PAIGNTON
TORRE   NEWTON ABBOT
PLYMOUTH (NORTH ROAD)

"CITY OF TRURO" 4-4-0 Locomotive

The City of Truro was built at Swindon Works in April 1903 and was distinguished by having attained a speed of 102.3 m.p.h. when working an Ocean Mail Special train between Plymouth and Bristol on 9th May, 1904.

In May 1931 this locomotive was placed in the York Railway Museum, but in January 1957 it was returned to the Western Region and is still performing useful service being in particular demand to convey special trains arranged for railway enthusiasts and party outings.

COMING SOON!
YOUR OWN
ITV STATION!

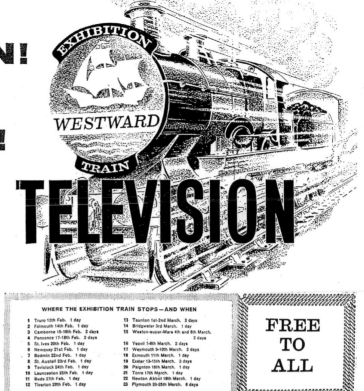

WESTWARD TELEVISION

On 29th April the West Country will have its own ITV Station

WESTWARD TELEVISION will bring you exciting new programmes — many of them with strong local interest — and ITV reception better than you have ever known before. Get ready *now*. Have your set converted so that you can enjoy this new experience in viewing!

VISIT THE WESTWARD EXHIBITION TRAIN

Come and see the Westward Exhibition Train, hauled by the famous veteran engine CITY OF TRURO (first engine to pull a train at 100 m.p.h.). It will be touring the West Country from 13th February till 25th March, stopping one day or more at 23 towns. The Exhibition Train will be in charge of Jack Train ('Colonel Chinstrap' to you). It will be declared open by the Mayor of each town. Famous Radio and TV personalities will make special personal appearances. Come and see extracts from the Films booked for the exciting new Westward programmes. Look in at the Candid Camera Interviews. See how easily *your* set can be converted to receive the Westward programmes — ITV reception at its best!

WHERE THE EXHIBITION TRAIN STOPS—AND WHEN

1	Truro 13th Feb. 1 day		13	Taunton 1st-2nd March. 2 days
2	Falmouth 14th Feb. 1 day		14	Bridgwater 3rd March. 1 day
3	Camborne 15-16th Feb. 2 days		15	Weston-super-Mare 4th and 6th March. 2 days
4	Penzance 17-18th Feb. 2 days		16	Yeovil 7-8th March. 2 days
5	St. Ives 20th Feb. 1 day		17	Weymouth 9-10th March. 2 days
6	Newquay 21st Feb. 1 day		18	Exmouth 11th March. 1 day
7	Bodmin 22nd Feb. 1 day		19	Exeter 13-15th March. 3 days
8	St. Austell 23rd Feb. 1 day		20	Paignton 16th March. 1 day
9	Tavistock 24th Feb. 1 day		21	Torre 17th March. 1 day
10	Launceston 25th Feb. 1 day		22	Newton Abbot 18th March. 1 day
11	Bude 27th Feb. 1 day		23	Plymouth 20-25th March. 6 days
12	Tiverton 28th Feb. 1 day			

FREE TO ALL

 HAVE YOUR SET CONVERTED WESTWARD NOW!

Order the new Westward Television magazine 'LOOK WESTWARD' from your newsagent now. Publication begins Tuesday, April 25th. Full details of Programmes and exciting Special Features.

---

by Rail with a Cheap Ticket
TO SEE THE
WESTWARD TELEVISION
EXHIBITION TRAIN

This special train, painted in the colours of Westward Television Ltd., has been arranged by the organisers as part of the campaign to publicise the opening of the Westward Television Plymouth Studio.

The train will consist of specially selected railway stock converted to provide a travelling cinema, a Transmitting Studio, and a comprehensive display of commercial exhibits.

It will be on exhibition at the following stations on the dates shown:—

STATION	DATE 1961
TRURO	Monday, 13th February
FALMOUTH	Tuesday, 14th February
CAMBORNE	Wednesday & Thursday, 15th & 16th February
PENZANCE	Friday & Saturday, 17th & 18th February
ST. IVES	Monday, 20th February
NEWQUAY	Tuesday, 21st February
BODMIN NORTH	Wednesday, 22nd February
ST. AUSTELL	Thursday, 23rd February
TAVISTOCK SOUTH	Friday, 24th February
LAUNCESTON	Saturday, 25th February
BUDE	Monday, 27th February
TIVERTON	Tuesday, 28th February
TAUNTON	Wednesday & Thursday, 1st & 2nd March
BRIDGWATER	Friday, 3rd March
WESTON-SUPER-MARE (Locking Road)	Saturday & Monday, 4th & 6th March
YEOVIL TOWN	Tuesday & Wednesday, 7th & 8th March
WEYMOUTH	Thursday & Friday, 9th & 10th March
EXMOUTH	Saturday, 11th March
EXETER CENTRAL	Mon., Tues. & Wed., 13th, 14th & 15th March
PAIGNTON	Thursday, 16th March
TORRE	Friday, 17th March
NEWTON ABBOT	Saturday, 18th March
PLYMOUTH (North Road)	Monday, 20th March to Saturday, 25th March

The Public will be admitted free to the above stations to view the Exhibition between 2 p.m.–9 p.m. daily.

British Railways will issue special Cheap Day Tickets from all stations within 30 miles of each exhibition point, in addition to their usual Excursion facilities.

— FULL DETAILS FROM —

Mr. D. S. Hart, Divisional Traffic Manager, Western Region, Transom House, Victoria Street, BRISTOL 1.

Mr. F. P. B. Taylor, Commercial Officer, Southern Region, Waterloo Station, LONDON, S.E.1.

BOOKING STATIONS AND AGENCIES OR FROM

WESTERN   SOUTHERN

---

staff who tried to ensure that the train arrived and departed punctually from all stops on its 1,200-mile route which, of course, the press could not refrain from dubbing a 'whistle-stop tour'. Many special arrangements had to be made by the Western Region, one typically requiring the train to be shunted no less than six times at a particular station to ensure that it was facing in the right direction and avoided disrupting normal passenger services. Other considerations were the transport and accommodation of over seventy train personnel from town to town, the decoration of stations with bunting and advertising paraphernalia, train cleaning, arrangement of opening receptions and catering for thousands of schoolchildren who came to visit the train. As for *City of Truro*, it was serviced at convenient sheds along the way.

At the various towns and cities visited it was the usual practice for a local civic dignitary to formally open the exhibition. This invariably meant a speech. At the train's first port of call in the South West – Truro, naturally – the Mayor of Truro, Mrs.Elsie Cornish, underlined the long wait for a second channel in the area: *'The West Country will now share in the facilities already enjoyed by the greater part of the country and as well as an advantage to ourselves I feel sure that the opportunity of viewing an alternative programme will be received with enthusiasm by our many visitors who have long been accustomed to this service.'* She continued: *'We have been twice honoured in this city for this is the inaugural opening and the engine pulling the train is the famous old locomotive the "City of Truro".'*

At Taunton, the mayor, Councillor Harnell, who was on record as having described television as a *'social evil'* at the annual conference of the Association of Municipal Corporations at Eastbourne, recanted somewhat in opening the Westward exhibition in his town: *'I think there has been a lot of nonsense talked about television. If Taunton people remember last September it seemed that the Mayor of Taunton was also talking nonsense about it.'* He added: *'I think there is a lot of good in television, and for those of you who think there is something bad about it, all you have to do is turn the set off.'* The Mayor of St.Ives, Councillor

The exhibition train visited Exeter Central on 13-15 March and, as was the custom throughout the tour, *City of Truro* itself was made accessible to visitors. The vehicle immediately behind the loco is the generator van. *Photograph courtesy S.P.Derek*

Another view of the exhibition train standing in Exeter Central goods yard. *Photograph courtesy E.S.Youldon*

The final stop on the tour was Plymouth North Road. Given that Plymouth was the largest centre of population served by the new television station (and, of course, that the TV station was based there!) it was unsurprising that this was also the longest stop of the tour, the train being on show there from 20-25 March. *Photograph courtesy G.E.Hemmett*

Norman Sanders, welcomed the competition that ITV would bring to '...*this remote corner of the British Empire*' and reflected that the BBC had been '*rather tardy*' in improving reception in West Cornwall, a situation which he hoped the arrival of an alternative station might remedy.

When it came to press reports, the *Exeter Express & Echo* seems to have been trying for a literary award – it waxed positively Shakespearian when describing the competition which the new television station would engender: '*Does BBC television (the reigning Ariel of the moment) regard the train as Caliban? Certainly, after April 29, when the Westward service begins, the threat of the "monster" train will give way to the actual competition of "spirit versus spirit" over the ether.*'

Famous radio and television personalities made special guest appearances *en route*. For the opening at Kensington Olympia Tommy Trinder was on hand, while in Torre, Richard Murdoch joined the show, and in Taunton the former British featherweight boxing champion, Bobby Neill, met the public, some 14,000 of whom turned up over the two days that the train was in the town. Coco the Clown, Billy Wright – with wife Joy of the Beverley Sisters – and Richard 'Mr.Pastry' Hearne all visited the train in Weston-super-Mare, where a procession of Weston's famous beach donkey carts was lined up outside the station giving children rides through the town. Elsewhere on the tour, fashion parades were staged on board and local talent was not forgotten with local group the Clubmen doing a turn in Taunton, Ricki Ford & The Cyclones providing what the

Weston Mercury described as a programme of 'pop numbers', and the Tone Valley Jazzband entertaining in Bridgwater. Even bad weather did not deter the crowds, the Cornish & Devon Post reporting that '...*it rained practically all day when the blue and white Television Train visited Bude on Monday, but this did not stop hundreds of people going along to see the exhibition.*'

According to an article in *The West Briton & Royal Cornwall Gazette* of 16 February 1961, '*Visitors to the train are greeted by charming hostesses and are then free to wander throughout the train at will. They can refresh themselves at the coffee bar; or rest in the reception coach. If they happen along at the right moment, they may well find themselves on the closed circuit television which operates throughout the train being interviewed by Jack Train* (the appropriately named actor and comedian who was the official host throughout the train's tour). *Mr.Train sits in a model studio and "nabs" his victims as they pass the door. While appearing on sets throughout the train, they can also watch themselves being interviewed on a monitor screen in front of them.*' This tactic no doubt intrigued the public and was a reflection of the highly popular 'Candid Camera' show. Jack Train himself had had a long and distinguished radio career based largely on his alter ego, the dipsomaniac 'Colonel Chinstrap' of BBC Radio's wartime ITMA (It's That Man Again) fame, his catch-phrase "I don't mind if I do" making him a national figure at the time. He also appeared in such shows as Twenty Questions and hosted record programmes, but he was no stranger to the new medium of television, as he had compèred the opening night of Westward's

neighbouring station, TWW, in 1958, and also appeared in a popular advertisement for chocolate.

By the time the train was coming towards the end of its tour at Paignton, the 150,000th visitor had been welcomed aboard and won a prize of a weekend in London for himself and family. Other prizes had been given out as the exhibition progressed around the region including TV sets, a weekend in Paris and, more bizarrely, free bacon and eggs for a year.

..........oooooOOOooooo..........

Westward's area covered the whole of Devon and Cornwall and large parts of Dorset and Somerset, and the publicity exercise cost some £35,000 to mount (approximately £500,000 at today's prices). Over 70% of the shares of the new company were owned by people living in these four counties. It was expected that Westward's Stockland Hill transmitter near Axminster would give some overlap in coverage with TWW which served Bristol and South Wales; in the event, the overlap was double that originally estimated with some 200,000 potential viewers being able to receive both stations, the signal being well received as far north as Bristol and across the Bristol Channel into Wales. This led to an uneasy relationship between the two companies which were, of course, competing for viewers and advertisers in the 'overlap' area, and this goes some way to explain the number of stops made by the train in the north and east of the franchise area. There certainly was rivalry. When visiting Weston-super-Mare, which could receive

FRIDAY   EXPRESS & ECHO   MARCH 10, 1961.

WESTWARD TELEVISION EXHIBITION TRAIN
VISITS EXETER MARCH 13th, 14th, and 15th

B.R. HELP I.TV TO ADVANCE EVER 'WESTWARD'

WESTWARD TELEVISION'S pre-arrival impact on the Westcountry owes much to British Railways. The company's first publicity onslaught has been made with an exhibition train, calling at most of the large towns in the area.

Does B.B.C. Television (the reigning Ariel of the moment) regard the train as a Caliban? Certainly after April 29, when the Westward service begins, the threat of the "monster" train will give way to the actual competition of "spirit versus spirit" over the ether.

Westward's train, pulled by the old City of Truro steam engine, consists of three coaches filled with exhibition stands, a studio coach, a reception coach (incorporating a small cinema), and a van containing the generator.

It is on a 1,000-mile whistle stop tour for six weeks, stopping at 23 major Westcountry towns, whose populations add up to nearly threequarter million.

Mr. Jack Train has been acting as the official host for the trip,

> The exhibition train will be at Exeter Central Station from March 13 to March 15. It has visited Tiverton, Taunton, and Bridgwater, and goes to Yeovil on March 7 and Newton Abbot on March 18.

and celebrities from the entertainment world are to travel down to visit the mobile exhibition.

Excerpts from some of the programmes to be presented when Westward goes on the air are being shown on television sets aboard the train.

both Westward and TWW, Peter Cadbury stated that he was all for competition and hoped that the two companies could co-exist on friendly terms, but when asked what he thought of TWW's studio map which showed coverage of the whole of the West Country, his blunt response was that he could not see the point of it, '...it being ridiculous for them to claim that they were serving the West of England.'

Westward was committed to providing some 5-6 hours of local programmes per week by September 1961, that figure eventually increasing to some 15-20% of total output. The initial home-grown productions included such gems as 'Ordinary People', a live evening quiz show with a main prize of £100, and 'Look in for Lunch' which was, as the name suggests, timed for 1pm daily, plus of course a local news bulletin at 6.05pm on Monday-Friday. A new weekly publication 'Look Westward' would be launched containing full details of all the new programmes. When addressing the Weston-super-Mare Rotary Club, Peter Cadbury said wryly that there were upwards of 1.5 million potential viewers in the region and that '...all but six of them have written to me to say what kind of programmes they want! We hope to please the majority of the people the majority of the time.' The new TV station also promised there would be '...less of the Wild West and more of the South West."

Other locomotives

As mentioned earlier, City of Truro did not haul the exhibition train on every stage of its journey. It handed over to indigenous motive power when visiting the Southern Region, and changes were also required when Truro's axleweight of 18½ tons was too heavy for a particular section of line. Among the changes was that for the Weymouth exhibition – T9 4-4-0 30120 took the train from Yeovil Town, where it had been

on show on March 7/8, to Weymouth for a couple of days, where 13,000 turned out to see the exhibition. Another change of motive power was seen at Exmouth; that leg of the tour on 11 March was handled by the equally venerable Adams 'Radial' 30582 which had recently been displaced from the Lyme Regis branch by Ivatt tanks. Incidentally, some 7,800 visitors were recorded at Exmouth. For the visit to Launceston, the train was brought in on the evening of 24 February by WR Prairie Tanks 5531 and 4570; T9 30120 was sent along from Exmouth Junction to provide steam heating during the exhibition the following day. A further change was seen at St.Ives. City of Truro was too heavy for the branch but, frustratingly, the substitute motive power for the trip from St.Erth to St.Ives seems to have gone unrecorded (though the obvious candidates would have been a pair of 45XX 2-6-2Ts). The local newspaper – clearly aware of City of Truro's celebrity status – commented: 'A disappointment for the many St.Ives people who flocked to see the travelling exhibition was the absence of the famous GWR locomotive City of Truro... which was too large to negotiate the curving single track from the mainline. It had to be left at St Erth, while a light (sic) engine hauled the television train to St Ives.'

Pictures of the train and coverage of the tour from a railway operating angle are very rare in both the

railway and general press, so we have been unable to determine whether City of Truro actually reached locations such as Bude (we are fairly sure that a T9 was used for that venue), Bodmin North and Tavistock. We would welcome information.

..........ooooo000ooooo..........

Somewhat ironically, Westward Television was to be outlived by City of Truro. Whereas the locomotive is still alive and very well, Westward Television survived for only 20 years. Although the station was popular with local viewers, there were problems upstairs: Peter Cadbury fell out with the IBA over an abortive plan for an airline company, 'Air Westward', and there were accusations that the Board too often made important decisions in London which was too remote from the area that the station was meant to be serving. By August 1981 Westward could no longer carry on and TSW stepped in to take over running of the station – albeit still under the Westward banner – until the formal start of their own franchise on 1 January 1982.

Acknowledgements: During the preparation of this article reference was made to contemporary issues of The West Briton & Royal Cornwall Gazette, Dorset Echo, St. Ives Gazette, Western Gazette, Weston Mercury, Cornish & Devon Post and The Exeter Express & Echo.

Reference was also made to a short (14-minute) film made by Westward TV featuring the opening at Olympia. Among the fascinating sequences is one of the Mayor of London making an address in which he sportingly mentions that he was part of a rival consortium for the franchise and in which he admits that he has been slow to own a TV set. He goes on to congratulate the organisers for coming up with the idea of a travelling train to reach as many of the potential audience as possible. He mentions, a touch gratefully, that the route of the exhibition train would not touch his neck of the woods as 'I myself live at a point that will not be reached by so much as 30 miles at least because the railway lines in one of the last corners of England that is still real country have not, I'm glad to say, crossed all the countryside yet.' *There then follows a tour of the train looking at a display of aerials and sets, many of which were made by Pye and Decca who took large sections of exhibition space, a model of the new Plymouth studios, and a photographic display of some of the big ITV stars of the time such as Patrick (Danger Man) McGoohan and Charlie Drake. The film also shows the Mayor being interviewed by Jack Train, signing the official visitor's book, visiting the footplate of* City of Truro *to meet the loco crew and looking at a poster of the first of the new* Look Westward *TV magazines (5d weekly), the cover picture of which featured none other than Richard (Robin Hood) Greene. VHS Video copies of this fascinating glimpse of the world of 1961 can be obtained from: South West Film & Television Archive, Royal William Yard, Stonehouse, Plymouth PL1 3RP.*

Top right. In terms of publicity, the exhibition train was a huge success. Wherever it went, the local media was there. This classic publicity shot of *City of Truro's* driver, Mr.Eric White of Bath Road depot, stopping Coco the Clown from advancing towards the loco was apparently taken during the train's visit to Weston-super-Mare. It will be noted in the itinerary that the exhibition at Weston was open on 4 and 6 March but not on the 5th; this was because the 5th was a Sunday, and on Sundays the engine and tour crew rested. *Photograph courtesy Colin White*

Below. For the Exmouth leg of the tour, the exhibition train was hauled by veteran Adams Radial Tank 30582. It was the usual practice for Southern locos to work the train on SR metals, but in the case of the Exmouth branch *City of Truro* would have been prohibited anyway because of its axleweight. Note that the headboard is a different (smaller) one than that attached to *City of Truro* in our earlier pictures. *Photograph: S.C.Nash; courtesy S.P.Derek*

Bottom right. Sporting the smaller headboard this time is the now-preserved T9 30120. It is seen with the exhibition train at Weymouth on 10 March. *Photograph: Colin Caddy collection*

LESS THAN CONVENTIONAL
Photographs by W.J.Ford

As *Bylines* readers will already know, some of the locomotives to be found in industrial service were, shall we say, a little less than conventional. The two specimens on this page certainly fall into that category. Our upper picture shows 'The Tank' – the English Electric battery locomotive which was used by Bowater's Lloyd on the 3ft gauge system at their paper mills at Sittingbourne. Delivered in 1921 principally for working at Ridham Dock, 'The Tank' could operate for eight hours on one battery charge. The machine remained in use until the closure of the paper mill's narrow gauge system in 1968. Our lower picture shows the four-wheeled locomotive which was used at the Castrol Oil Depot at Hayes, Middlesex, from 1934 until 1962. The loco is stated to have been built by E.E.Baguley of Burton-on-Trent, but we have not been able to determine whether all of it was built by that firm or whether they merely supplied the power unit for mounting on to what looks like a modified wagon frame. Another grey area concerns the machine's fate; following the cessation of rail traffic at the Hayes depot in 1962 the loco is thought to have been transferred to Castrol's depot at Stanlow, Cheshire, but we not been able to find any confirmation of that transfer.

REACHING NEW HEIGHTS – a quartet of cranes
Photographs courtesy of the Bodmin & Wenford Railway Trust; notes by Steve Daly

1

Over the centuries men have found that mechanical aids take the effort out of many routine tasks, such as lifting or moving heavy loads. Our early ancestors developed rudimentary cranes and lifting tackle and these were further developed and improved as the years progressed. By the time railways appeared on the scene the usefulness of such equipment had been very well proven, so it was understandable that the railway companies adapted and used cranes for a variety of purposes. Most, but not all, goods yards contained at least one crane. However, these suffered from at least two disadvantages: firstly, they were usually fixed in one location and secondly, they were often of limited lifting capacity, the most common being no more than one or two tons. In order to overcome the first limitation, the crane manufacturers collaborated with the commercial motor builders to develop mobile cranes; the collaboration was such that the crane companies' greatest customers for mobile pieces of lifting equipment were the railways. Furthermore, mobile cranes could be moved from one yard to another, wherever and whenever they were needed. Here we have four examples of mobile cranes in service with the London, Midland

& Scottish Railway. Our first subject (**photograph 1**) is a product of Walker Brothers. Situated between Wigan and Gathurst on the Lancashire & Yorkshire line from Wigan (Wallgate) to Southport (Chapel Street), the Walker Brothers factory had its own railway connection known variously as Pagefield Siding or Pagefield Forge Siding. We are looking at a 6-ton crane which was produced for the LMS in 1929. Mounted on a Pagefield chassis – which was also built by Walkers – it was powered by a Dorman petrol engine and had a Tilling Stevens Electric transmission. This vehicle carries the fleet number 42X, the 'X' suffix being used by the LMS for miscellaneous vehicles which did not fit anywhere else in its numbering system. The vehicle is seen loading a 'BX' type container on to the back of an AEC 'Y' type lorry; the lorry has the fleet number 526B and is carrying a demountable flat-bed body number 5004B. The location is Somers Town goods yard, near St. Pancras station. We can see from this photograph that the crane driver was able to swivel his seat through 180° from the normal driving position. Also of note is the fact that the crane is fitted with solid tyres, while the lorry it is loading is running on pneumatic tyres.

In **photograph 2** we have another Walker Brothers crane. This one is mounted on a lorry chassis and is driven from the lorry cab itself; this was something of a disadvantage as it meant that the driver's view was completely obstructed for the majority of the crane's traverse. The crane is in the process of lifting a 'B' type container from its wagon. It has clearly been worked hard – note the extremely battered mudguards and the score marks on the crane's counterweight. The container itself appears to be of steel construction of a similar design to the Butterley patent all-steel container built for the GWR in 1929 and condemned during World War Two. Unfortunately we are unable to tell you where this little cameo was photographed.

The next subject, **photograph 3**, is a later model of container crane, this time from the well-known Ipswich company of Ransome & Rapier. This example has much in common with the Walker crane seen previously, but it is mounted rigidly and does not have a traverse. The short wheelbase gave it the manoeuvrability that was required to compensate for the lack of traverse. However, this design still suffered disadvantages in that while the load and the jib were always within the

2

3

7253 stands partly in, partly out of Laxfield shed on the Mid-Suffolk Light Railway on 5 July 1936. Given the severely restricted height of the shed entrance, we suspect that the loco's chimney could not actually have fitted inside the building. Note that 7253's handrail is continuous along the boiler and around the top of the smokebox. As noted in the text, the J65s were the mainstay of 'Middy' motive power from the mid-1920s to the latter part of the 1940s. *Photograph: H.C.Casserley*

were formed of four six-wheelers. Even after the Great War the Blackwall line still had an intensive service at 15-minute intervals between 7am and 8pm; this was despite competition from electrified tram services. However, in the 1920s the line's fortunes started to significantly decline and the drastic drop in passenger traffic during the General Strike proved to be the proverbial nail in the coffin, the last passenger trains running on 3 May 1926. Although this made the J65s redundant, it is thought that some were kept on at the parent shed at Stratford for shunting and local goods turns; indeed there is photographic evidence of 7155 and 7249 in 'The Field' at the back of the shed – they were in company with a number of other Stratford 0-6-0Ts, 2-4-2Ts and a J15 – as late as June 1936, though the engines were sheeted down.

Colchester and its sub-sheds: Although Colchester often had several E22s/J65s, prior to the Grouping most of the engines were usually out-stationed at one of the sub-sheds. Indeed, two of the engines – GER 155 and 156 – had gone new to the sub-shed at Braintree in 1889. As far as can be determined the E22s/J65s were used on the Witham-Braintree-Bishops Stortford line prior to the arrival of small 2-4-2Ts in 1910. To the south of Colchester, the sub-shed at Maldon had a solitary J65, 7151, in 1934, presumably for the sparse service on the line from Maldon (West) to Woodham Ferrers.

It might be assumed that, as the J65s were very lightweight engines, they would have been the obvious choices for the Kelvedon, Tollesbury & Tiptree Light

Railway, which was worked by the GER and subsequently the LNER, a Colchester engine being outstationed at the small sub-shed at Kelvedon. Surprisingly, though, despite the fact that the Tollesbury line was restricted to engines with an 'Unclassified' Route Availabilty, there is no record that the E22/J65s were ever used on it.

After the Grouping Colchester's J65s found an additional source of work on the Colne Valley & Halstead Railway. Prior to the Grouping this independent concern had used its own locomotives; the passenger traffic had been in the hands of its three Hawthorn Leslie 2-4-2Ts, but all three were scrapped between 1923 and 1930 and J65s were the ideal substitutes

J65 0-6-0Ts – summary of class
All built at Stratford; numbers in brackets not carried

GER No.	First LNER No.	1946 No.	BR No. (date applied)	Built	Vacuum fitted	Withdrawn
150	7150	-	-	2.1889	10.1925	6.1937
151	7151	-	-	2.1889	10.1931	7.1937
152	7152		-	2.1889	-	10.1935
153	7153		-	2.1889	-	9.1931
154	7154	-	-	2.1889	-	4.1932
155	7155	8211	**68211** (3.51)	2.1889	-	11.1953
156	7156	-	-	3.1889	10.1931	8.1937
157	7157	8212	-	3.1889	-	11.1947
158	7158	-	-	3.1889	-	3.1932
159	7159	-	-	6.1889	-	5.1937
245	7245	-	-	2.1893	-	1.1931
246	7246	-	-	2.1893	-	12.1930
247	7247	8213	**(68213)**	2.1893	-	2.1948
248	7248	-	-	3.1893	11.1925	5.1936
249	7249	-	-	3.1893	-	7.1937
250	7250	8214	**68214** (8.51)	3.1893	9.1925	10.1956
251	7251	-	-	3.1893	9.1925	12.1931
252	7252	-	-	3.1893	10.1925	8.1935
253	7253	8215	**(68215)**	4.1893	-	5.1949
254	7254	-	-	4.1893	9.1924	6.1937

Stovepipe-chimneyed 7247 on the 'Middy' in the early 1930s – it is standing at Laxfield, having brought in a train from Haughley. *Photograph: Dr.Ian C.Allen; The Transport Treasury*

on this lightly-laid line. However, the replacement of the CV&HR's flat-bottomed track in 1934 enabled slightly heavier locomotives to be used, and the J65s were ousted by J15 0-6-0s.

Parkeston: In early LNER days Parkeston usually had five or six J65s and as many were still in use there until mid-1937. Indeed, 7250 remained for even longer, no doubt as a 'spare' engine. It should be remembered that in addition to the large passenger terminal at Parkeston which was used by ships from Scandinavia and the Low Countries, a few miles along the line was Harwich which itself remained a flourishing port, its importance enhanced by the Train Ferry service to Zeebrugge which was inaugurated in April 1924. There had always been plenty of work for the small 0-6-0Ts, shunting the quays at Harwich Town and heading the frequent passenger service provided between Harwich and Parkeston Quay, primarily for the dock workers. It is clear that the requirement for a number of J65 to be dual-fitted in 1924/25 had arisen out of the increase of freight traffic associated with the Train Ferries, and it will be seen from the accompanying table that the engines recorded as allocated to Parkeston in the 1930s were, without exception, vacuum-fitted.

Ipswich and its sub-sheds: There were always several of the class allocated to Ipswich. Those based at the parent shed worked alongside J70 tram engines on shunting in the dock sidings along the River Orwell. Indeed, the penultimate survivor – 68211 – was at Ipswich until withdrawn in November 1953, latterly being fitted with a spark arrester and working as a 2-4-0T with the front sections of its rods removed. Following the arrival of diesel shunters at Ipswich from May 1952 onwards, the services of the J65 were dispensed with.

From the 1890s, an Ipswich J65 was usually outstationed at Eye to work the passenger service on the short branch from Mellis. The use of a J65 was not in this case due to the lightness of the track, but to the lightness of the traffic, for which two six-wheelers sufficed. This sparsely-used branch lost its passenger services in February 1931 so the J65s' association with the line came to an end. Although the branch remained open to goods traffic until July 1964, J17 0-6-0s were the usual engines for these duties.

In common with Colchester shed, Ipswich gained another duty for its J65s after the Grouping. In this case it was the Mid-Suffolk Light Railway, which was taken into the LNER fold on 1 July 1924. Like the Colne Valley & Halstead line, the Mid-Suffolk had had its own locomotives – in this case three Hudswell Clarke 0-6-0Ts – but all three were scrapped in the 1920s and were replaced by J65s, one or two of which were out-stationed at the ramshackle ex-Mid-Suffolk shed at Laxfield. It should be noted that, even before the Grouping, the E22s/J65s had been used on the Mid-Suffolk, the Great Eastern having helped out the little company when the latter's locomotives were under repair. In the Summer of 1919, for example, 157 and 254 were both supplied during a crisis when two of the Mid-Suffolk engines were out of action. 247 was similarly used during September 1920.

The J65s' association with the Mid-Suffolk was such that, over the years, 7153, 7156, 7157, 7247, 7250, 7253 and 7254 were all used on the line at one time or another. Furthermore, by the end of 1937, when only five of the class remained, four of them – 7155, 7157, 7247 and 7253 – were all at Ipswich, either shunting at the docks or working on the Mid-Suffolk line. However, during 1947 all the old flat-bottomed track on the Mid-Suffolk was replaced, and this enabled J15 0-6-0s to take over from the J65s. The last recorded appearance of a J65 on the Mid-Suffolk was in May 1948, when 8211 worked the passenger services for two weeks.

Cambridge and its sub-sheds: Shortly after the completion of the second batch of ten E22s, Cambridge received an allocation of three of the class. One was sub-shedded at Stoke Ferry and another at Saffron Walden, while the third was a 'spare' for these duties. This remained the usual scenario until shortly after the Grouping.

Of the E22s/J65s used on the Stoke Ferry branch, 150, in particular, was associated with the line – and the little shed at the terminus – for many years, but

'2-4-0T' 68211 stands at Ipswich shed yard some time in 1951/52. The rest of the line-up is typical Ipswich – a Framlingham branch F6 2-4-2T, a B1, a J15 and a J17. *Photograph: Dr.Ian C.Allen; The Transport Treasury*

The last survivor, 68214, stands at Yarmouth Beach shed yard. The houses in the background front on to Wellesley Road. Note that the loco has a mix of 'solid' and crescent-shaped balance weights and that its Ross Pop safety valves are mounted directly on to the boiler. In common with some of the other engines pictured in this article, its toolbox has been removed from the top of the tank. *Photograph: Dr.Ian C.Allen; The Transport Treasury*

SHROPSHIRE & MONTGOMERYSHIRE MISCELLANY

Colonel Stephens' motto might well have been 'Throw Nothing Away', and that motto seemed to linger. Even twenty or more years after the Colonel had passed to the Great Light Railway in the Sky, a fascinating assortment of long-abandoned bits and pieces could still be found on railways which had once formed part of his charismatic empire. The old Shropshire & Montgomeryshire was just one railway where the long-since disused still languished. This item is the remains of the S&M's Wolseley-Siddeley railbus. After the railbus had finished work in the mid-1930s the body had removed and altered and fitted to a chassis for use as an inspection saloon, hauled by the S&M's famous 0-4-2WT *Gazelle*. However, the 'reconfigured' coach gave up the ghost during the war and the body was removed and used as a platelayer's hut at Kinnerley Junction. This was how it looked on 25 April 1954. It remained *in situ* for another thirty years or so, thereby out-living the S&M by almost three decades. *Photograph: F.W.Shuttleworth*

Another item of Shropshire & Montgomeryshire exotica was their coach No.1A, a small four-wheeler which had been built in 1843 as part of the L&SWR's Royal Train. The S&M purchased it third-hand in the mid-1920s and it remained in use until 1953, albeit latterly as part of the breakdown train. The Army – who by then controlled the S&M – took it to Longmoor with the intention of preserving it but, unfortunately, the vehicle was considered to be too far gone and was therefore scrapped. This picture of the once-grand Royal coach was taken at Kinnerley Junction on 21 June 1947. *Photograph: H.C.Casserley*

It was fairly common practice on the railways for discarded items of rolling stock to be put to some use or other, but in most cases the 'recycled' vehicles were finally disposed of before they became too derelict. But that was not how things were done on the Colonel Stephens railways. As evidenced here, former S&M van No.18 remained in use as a bothy despite having become positively ramshackle. This wooden-bodied van is thought to have come from the Midland Railway; it was photographed at its final resting place at Kinnerley Junction on 21 September 1958. Note the chimney and note also the grindstone (no – it is *not* a tombola tumbler) on the left. *Photograph: R.M.Casserley*

The photographer's rummage around the S&M on 21 September 1958 was courtesy of one of several rail tours which visited the line in that decade. This tour took in the Criggion branch but, because of the condition of the track on the branch and the strict weight limit over Melverley Viaduct, steam locos were not permitted on that section; so the Criggion leg was done in one of the Army's Wickham Trolleys. Here we see the trolley standing at Melverley station, the small platform of which is visible through the centre arch of the disproportionately extravagant road bridge. *Photograph: R.M.Casserley*

At its western end, the S&M joined the former Cambrian Railways' Oswestry-Welshpool line at Llanymynech. As the station there had to cater, not only for the S&M, but also for passengers on the ex-Cambrian line, it remained active long after the S&M had closed its doors to passengers. When the station buildings were photographed on 14 September 1956 they looked as if they had recently had a visit from the decorators. Nevertheless, class distinctions had not been dispensed with – First Class and Third Class passengers still had separate refreshment facilities. (Or does the First Class and Third Class refer to the quality of refreshments? No, let's not be silly.) *Photograph: H.C.Casserley*

By the time this picture of the station building at Kinnerley Junction was taken on 21 June 1947, it had been more than fourteen years since the premises had had to deal with any 'ordinary' public passenger and parcels traffic. Nevertheless, one of the old notices remained: the 'parcels' notice, the almost-indistinct bottom line of which reads 'Support Your Local Line'. The uncharacteristically substantial construction of the station building – bricks and roof slates instead of the usual S&M timber – was a left-over from the days of 'The Potts' (the Potteries, Shrewsbury & North Wales Railway) which had built the original line in 1866. *Photograph: H.C.Casserley*

A somewhat surreal sight for the unsuspecting visitor to Llanymynech station in 1954 was a former Manchester, Sheffield & Lincolnshire Railway six-wheeled coach (possibly a luggage third) painted in the station colours of light green and cream. The coach was in the yard which, in later years at least, was used by the North Wales Wagon Company for the breaking up of condemned wagons. This picture, which was taken on 25 April 1954, shows the coach in splendid cosmetic condition, Now read on... *Photograph: F.W.Shuttleworth*

Only a little over four years later – on 20 September 1958 – the once-impressive ex-MS&L coach at Llanymynech had deteriorated to this. What a tragedy. However, rolling stock enthusiasts visiting the station had a new item of interest; this was the GWR railmotor trailer W210, which had been condemned in November 1956. It is seen lurking in the background on the right. The trailer was still at the station until at least 1962; it served as an office and mess room for the North Wales Wagon Company which, in the early 1960s, was very busy indeed cutting up wagons, carriages and at least one locomotive (WR 2-8-0 2869). *Photograph: H.C.Casserley*

QUAKERS YARD

A selection of historical notes and recollections of a South Wales valleys junction and its railway neighbours

by Edward A. Evans

In early 1958 my colleagues and I discovered a few dozen two-colour pamphlets rammed into the booking office publicity rack at our local station. The pamphlets depicted the new Derby-built diesel multiple units that were being introduced to the valleys of South Wales in the hope of providing improved services. The pamphlets immediately aroused our curiosity. Here, I should point out that I use the words 'we' and 'our' because I, along with three friends, had formed an unofficial railway club. Pocket money permitting, we travelled extensively on our local lines. We weren't trainspotters in the accepted sense; none of us was a number-taker. We preferred to observe the general railway scene. As schoolboys, most of our observing was done between Aberdare (High Level) and Pontypool Road on the Vale of Neath line, the branch to Dowlais (Cae Harris) and the ex-TVR line from Cardiff to Merthyr. Two of us followed the fortunes of Cardiff City which meant we made frequent trips on Rhymney-Cardiff soccer specials to Ninian Park Platform.

The discovery of the pamphlets provided us with a hint that there was something new on the horizon. They depicted a gleaming diesel multiple unit, complete with a speed-whisker across its front. We were told by the station clerk that the new diesels would probably not be seen on the Vale of Neath line and that we would have to travel to Quakers Yard to observe them.

So it was in springtime, to satisfy our curiosity, that we booked half returns for the 2¼-mile journey to Quakers Yard. We had passed through the station several times en route to Aberdare, but this was the first time we had alighted. The new diesel multiple units were a novelty. The most notable feature – apart from the speed-whisker – was the airiness of the train's compartments and the splendid view one could obtain from a seat behind the driver.

Having surmounted the mighty 1 in 38 bank from Abercynon, the DMU came to a vibrating stand at the up platform of Low Level. With station work completed, it grumbled its way around the curves north of the station and was soon rattling its way to Merthyr. We hung around for a pleasant hour or so in the hope of seeing the DMU on its return trip. It was during that time on a pleasant, lazy Saturday afternoon that it occurred to me that Quakers Yard was a special place in the network of railways that served the valleys of South Wales.

As the years passed, I got to know the station quite well. The narrative which

Left. Quakers Yard High Level station – 6649 stands at the head of the 1.05pm Pontypool Road-Neath on 11 April 1955. *Photograph: R.M.Casserley*

follows will, I hope, tell the story of how Quakers Yard developed into a busy junction – a railway crossroads – and how its decline began in the early 1950s.

The background

The standard gauge railway was not the first form of transport to make its mark on Quakers Yard. To the west, on the slopes of Cefn Glas, the Glamorganshire Canal opened on 10 February 1794 to link Merthyr with Cardiff, followed the curving contour of the hillside. On the east bank of the River Taff, the 4ft 2in gauge Penydarren (or Merthyr) Tramroad, upon which Richard Trevithick's locomotive made its historic run from Merthyr to Navigation House in 1804, kept close company with the river.

To those not familiar with the upper Taff Valley in Glamorgan, it should be understood that Quakers Yard station is not *in* Quakers Yard! This strange state of affairs came about with the coming of the Taff Vale Railway (TVR) which took the form of a single line from Cardiff to Merthyr. The main line had, at first, run as far as Navigation House (Abercynon). With the completion of the main incline above Navigation, a viaduct over the River Taff, and various engineering works nearer Merthyr, the line was open throughout for traffic on 21 April 1841. *(Most sources give the date of opening as 12 April, but the 21st is confirmed in contemporary issues of the* Monmouthshire Merlin *– Ed.)*

For seventeen years the TVR main line, once it had crossed the viaduct, wound its way through unspoilt countryside to travel along the east bank of the river to the terminus at Merthyr Tydfil. In 1858, the Newport Abergavenny & Hereford Railway (NAHR) completed its Taff Vale Extension Railway from Pontypool to connect with the TVR at a location eight miles south of Merthyr Tydfil. The connection between the two railways was made on sloping ground below the Merthyr-Cardiff turnpike road. At the time, the nearest hamlet of any size was Quakers Yard, on the River Taff, one mile away to the south-east. A station was opened on 5 January 1858 by the TVR – and was used by the NAHR – for the interchange of passengers. The station took its name from the nearest settlement of note at the time, which happened to be Quakers Yard. (The villages of Treharris and Edwardsville, although closer to the railway, did not exist at the time the railway arrived – more of this anon.) Quakers Yard is mentioned in George Borrow's *Wild Wales* and at the time of the coming of the TVR was nothing more than a cluster of tiny cottages on the east bank of the river and a toll house and a few more minuscule dwellings on the opposite bank. The village took its name from a Society of Friends' burial ground – hence the name Quakers Yard.

Mention was made of Treharris. In the latter years of the nineteenth century the neighbouring village of Treharris (Harris' Town) was founded following the sinking of Harris' Deep Navigation Colliery. In its

heyday Treharris was a bustling place. Every piece of available ground was used to provide colliery workers with living accommodation. Half a mile to the west a new village was established. It was intended as an overspill for Treharris and new terraced houses were built near Quakers Yard Junction. A building society was formed to finance the construction of the houses and a meeting was held in the Great Western Hotel, adjacent to the junction, to decide on a name for this village. Several suggestions were made, but it was the casting vote of the society's chairman, Edmund Edwards, that finally decided the matter. The chairman's surname is significant: the village was called Edwardsville. Thus, the station that was known, and is still known, as Quakers Yard, by sheer fluke of its location in its early days, actually stands in the later village of Edwardsville.

In explaining the odd location of the station I have moved forward by about forty years so to continue the story in its correct sequence, I must return to the 1850s. The development of Quakers Yard as a railway installation can at first appear a little confusing as expansion commenced in 1858 and continued apace for the next three decades, turning the place into a railway crossroads of considerable interest. Its development is best summarised as follows:

1858: On 11 January Quakers Yard became a junction with the completion, from the east, of the NAHR's Taff Vale Extension Railway. (The NAHR was absorbed by the West Midland Railway in 1860; the West Midland was in turn absorbed by the GWR in 1863.)

1863: The widening of the Taff Vale viaduct, which was to meet the increased demands of traffic on the TVR main line, was completed in February of this year. At the same time as this work was carried out, the tunnel at Pen Locks was opened out into a cutting to accept the second line of rails. (The name 'Pen Locks' was the local name for Top Locks which was just south of the viaduct.) Material excavated from the cutting was used to widen the viaduct. The completion date of this work is set in stone in the parapet of the viaduct.

1864: The former NAHR line (now GWR) was extended from Quakers Yard East Junction, across the River Taff by a viaduct and through Cefn Glas Tunnel into the Aberdare Valley. It opened to passengers on 5 October. At Middle Duffryn (Abercwmboi) it made an end-on junction with the Vale of Neath Railway. Thus a continuous through route was created between Pontypool and Neath, the line being referred to as the Vale of Neath line. At Quakers Yard, the section between East Junction and Low Level Junction became known as the Quakers Yard Branch. The GWR opened a new station at Quakers Yard; it later became known as High Level to distinguish it from the original TVR station at Low Level. It initially comprised only a single platform, but that was soon found to be inadequate and as early as 26

QUAKERS YARD

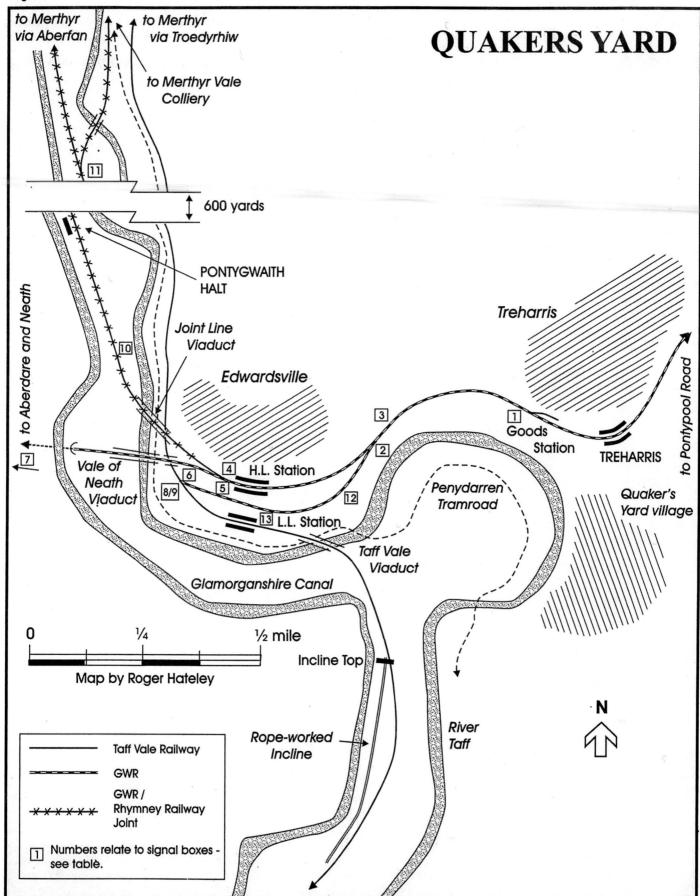

to Merthyr via Aberfan

to Merthyr via Troedyrhiw

to Merthyr Vale Colliery

11

600 yards

PONTYGWAITH HALT

to Aberdare and Neath

Joint Line Viaduct

Treharris

Edwardsville

10

3

1

Goods Station

to Pontypool Road

2

7

Vale of Neath Viaduct

4 H.L. Station

6

5

12

TREHARRIS

Quaker's Yard village

8/9

13 L.L. Station

Penydarren Tramroad

Taff Vale Viaduct

Glamorganshire Canal

0   ¼   ½ mile

Map by Roger Hateley

Incline Top

Rope-worked Incline

River Taff

N

Taff Vale Railway

GWR

GWR / Rhymney Railway Joint

1 Numbers relate to signal boxes – see table.

October 1864 the GWR Traffic Committee recommended that an additional platform should be provided. The recommendation was approved and the grand sum of £43 was sanctioned for the platform's construction.

1867: The main incline between Navigation House and Pen Locks was finally abandoned by the TVR in favour of a locomotive-worked line of 1 in 38.

1886: The Quakers Yard & Merthyr Joint line (GWR/Rhymney Railway), from High Level to Merthyr, via Aberfan and Abercanaid opened to passenger traffic on 1 April; (it had been open to mineral traffic since 31 December 1884). There were now two lines running from Quakers Yard to Merthyr – one on each side of the valley.

The Quakers Yard and Merthyr Joint line

As noted above, the Quakers Yard & Merthyr Joint line from Quakers Yard (High Level) to Merthyr was formally opened for passenger and freight traffic on 1 April 1886 but had been used by the Rhymney Railway from 31 December 1884 for occasional mineral traffic to the Cyfarthfa Works at Merthyr. Intermediate

Looking up from the Low Level to the High Level; the date is 26 September 1960. Most of the buildings at High Level were of timber construction whereas those at Low Level were of masonry. *Photograph: H.C.Casserley*

However, it is unclear whether the buildings which stood at both stations were provided at the time the stations first opened or whether they were added later. The following extracts from GWR Directors' Minutes and TVR Board Minutes offer a few clues:

TVR Board Minutes, 25 November 1870: *'The GWR Directors also alluded to the absolute necessity for the erection of a joint station at QY which was admitted by the TV Directors. They also resolved that the Board approve all these proceedings and that the Co contribute a moiety of the same of about £500 for the erection of a station at Quakers Yard.'* The GWR Directors' Minutes for 30 November 1870 confirm: *'...expenditure was authorised...new station at Quakers Yard jointly with the TV Co...£500.'*

There were further entries – 3 December 1879: *'Joint expenditure of £520 for alterations at Quakers Yard station authorised';* 7 April 1880: *'Further joint expenditure of £83 13s authorised';* GWR Directors' Minute, 12 October 1922: *'Provision of central booking office authorised.'* This 'central' booking office for both stations was at High Level – this was logical for such a facility as Low Level could be reached only by the footbridge from High Level. From this it can be safely assumed that prior to the Grouping both companies maintained their own booking facilities.

Little is known of the position of Station Master, particularly in the early days of Quakers Yard, but it is doubtful that there was a Station Master for each station. It is quite possible that an agreement was reached by the GWR and TVR whereby one man took responsibility for both stations. (The author would be interested to hear from anyone who can shed light upon this particular subject.)

Neighbours
At this point it is worth including a selection of notes on some of Quakers Yard's railway neighbours.

On the Joint Line, Pontygwaith Halt was brought into use on 11 September 1933. The halt, on the north side of Joint Line viaduct and 58 chains from High Level station, consisted of two timber platforms. Paths from each platform led up to an adjacent minor road overbridge. The halt served an isolated community which consisted of a row of ten stone and slate terraced houses, a few cottages and a couple of farms. One of the cottages was named 'Buarth Glas' (Blue Yard) and was the home of a lengthman. A journey on an auto-train from Pontygwaith to High Level took less then three minutes.

Heading east from Quakers Yard on the Vale of Neath line, the first stop was Treharris. Built on a sharp curve, Treharris station was opened to the public on 2 June 1890, at a time when the town was expanding following the earlier sinking of Deep Navigation Colliery. Limitations on available space meant that the booking office had to be located at a higher level adjacent to the Thomas Street overbridge. In its later years, and up until closure, Treharris was supervised by the Quakers Yard station master. Mr.Jack Lewis, the last incumbent at Quakers Yard, visited Treharris station twice a week. The station had a staff of three which consisted of a female Clerk and two Leading Porters.

During Treharris's 75 year history on the railway map, the station witnessed a number of special occasions which attracted onlookers in large numbers. Several Royal Trains passed through the station but probably the best remembered was the Royal Train of 25th July 1958 as this train actually stopped at the station for HRH The Duke of Edinburgh to alight and continue his journey to Merthyr Tydfil by road.

Around the curves to the west of the station stood Treharris Goods. Quakers Yard was not provided with a traditional goods yard for the receipt and despatch of general rail-borne merchandise; consequently, Treharris Goods served both stations as there was less than a mile

between the two. A stone-built goods shed was provided and this stood on a loop on the up side of the Vale of Neath line. The small yard was capable of handling livestock and parcels and was equipped with a one-ton capacity hand crane. With space at a premium the goods yard was situated in the most awkward location imaginable. In the days before the internal combustion engine one could only pity the poor horse that was required to haul a loaded four-wheeled delivery cart from the goods yard to the main thoroughfare in Perrott Street. To reach the latter, the horse was required to surmount the cruelly steep Prosser Street, a distance of about sixty yards. To ease the animal's burden over this short stretch, a second horse was used. This animal was known as a 'chain horse' and was attached to the cart by means of a chain and provided assistance to the 'wagon horse'. Thus the burden was shared until level Perrott Street was reached.

Treharris Goods was once a busy place, but towards the end parcels and general merchandise traffic dwindled. Deliveries from Treharris were undertaken on selected days of the week, or when required, by a driver using a Thorneycroft lorry based at Pontypridd Goods. Treharris Goods closed to ordinary goods traffic on 7 October 1963.

Danger – subsidence!

The most attractive features of the landscape around Quakers Yard were the viaducts. When built they were the most graceful of structures and from the early 20th century attracted professional photographers, notably those who produced picture postcards. Scores of photographs were taken of the three viaducts, but the Vale of Neath viaduct and the Joint Line viaduct had the greater coverage as they were more accessible and within a short distance of each other. Taff Vale viaduct was, and still is, difficult to photograph owing to its location in a narrow gorge through which the River Taff gushes on its way to the Bristol Channel.

In 1919 it was discovered that subsidence was causing havoc in the area around Quakers Yard. The problem was attributed to the amount of mining that had taken place in the locality, particularly in the areas directly beneath the viaducts. As a precaution, and for the safety of railway traffic, the three viaducts were reinforced by the placing of stout timbers in each of the arches. Thus the viaducts became curiosities and attracted a new generation of photographers.

The Vale of Neath viaduct and the Joint Line viaduct remained in this state until

the end of their useful working lives and beyond until demolition. The Taff Vale viaduct must have been considered by engineers to be stable enough as the timbers were removed in August 1955. This suggests that although the Vale of Neath and Joint Line viaducts had required reinforcement back in 1919, the similar treatment to the Taff Vale viaduct had been purely precautionary.

Quakers Yard East Junction

In 1864 the original section of the Extension Railway from East Junction to Low Level Junction became the Quakers Yard Branch. It was 50 chains (1,100 yards) in length. The first signal box to be established for the control of East Junction was Quakers Yard No.1 Junction, situated on the Down* side and within a few feet of the junction itself. Little is known of this box but records show that it was in use in by April 1877. About 14 chains to the east stood Treharris signal box. Again, little is known of this box other than that it had been opened by September 1886; also sited on the Down side, its purpose was to control traffic into the small goods yard opposite. In 1904 the abovementioned boxes were closed by the GWR and replaced by Quakers Yard East Junction box which

Left. Looking out from the Low Level station in the direction of Merthyr, February 1961. Low Level signal box can be seen. The tracks on the far right are those descending from the Vale of Neath line. The bridge in the distance carries that line. *Photograph: Peter Barnfield*

Below. Another north-westerly view along the Low Level station, this time on 15 July 1959. The 'hump' part-way along the Down (Cardiff) platform betrays where it was at one time lengthened. Note the pagoda waiting shelter on the Up platform and the chimneys of the ornate TVR building on the Down. *Photograph: H.C.Casserley*

stood on the Up side. It was positioned centrally on a tight curve and gave the signalman a commanding view not only of the junction, but also in both directions as far as the overbridge at Treharris station to the east, and within a few yards of High Level station to the west. A ground frame was provided for access to Treharris goods yard. *(* In contrast to the usual scenario where 'Up' meant towards London and 'Down' meant from London, in the Cardiff Valleys Up meant 'up' the valley – i.e. away from Cardiff – and Down meant 'down' the valley towards Cardiff.)*

The Quakers Yard branch itself proved a useful connection between the GWR and TVR and along its length sidings were laid – two on the Up side and one on the Down. At the top end of the branch a turntable was installed but was removed by 1919. Coal trains were marshalled on the branch for dispatch along the Vale of Neath line. Its busiest time seems to have been in the pre-Grouping period with regular trainloads from Merthyr Vale Colliery. The yard was quieter in later years but still busy enough to employ resident shunters. During the 1950s, for instance, two wagon examiners were employed in the yard, one man on each shift. At the site of the turntable were a couple of short sidings where wagon repairs were carried out. There was enough work for the employment of two wagon repairers on a permanent basis.

Accidents to railway personnel, it seems, were few and far between at Quakers Yard. But one that did occur, at East Junction, was particularly tragic. The event was related to me by a lampman attached to Quakers Yard during the late 1950s. He told me that a ganger was walking alongside the up line near East Junction; the ganger was an experienced man with many years' service but it is thought that, on the day in question, he had somehow forgotten *where* he was actually walking. An early morning passenger train from Aberdare to Ystrad Mynach, having made a punctual and spirited start from High Level, made its way around the curves towards Treharris. To the driver of the train – an Aberdare man of unblemished record – it was a routine trip and everything appeared quite normal. He made his usual stops at Treharris, Trelewis Halt and Nelson & Llancaiach. His next stop was Ystrad Mynach where he was met by a grim-faced railway official with the news that a man had been killed by his train at Quakers Yard East Junction. The shocked driver was immediately relieved of his duties at Ystrad Mynach and never drove a locomotive again. The enquiry into the accident was held at Nelson.

To round off this short account of the Quakers Yard branch, it is interesting to note here that when enginemen were taking a train off the Vale of Neath line

Looking in a south-easterly direction along the Up (northbound) platform at Low Level, 30 November 1957. *Photograph: R.M.Casserley*

and down the branch to Low Level they invariably stated that they were 'going down the hole'. I have heard this term many times but its origin remains a mystery.

Staffing, 1950s

Although a rather sizeable railway installation, Quakers Yard was not provided with a station house. The last Station Master, Mr.Jack Lewis, commuted daily from his home at Aberdare. His predecessor, a Mr.Wilkinson, lodged in a house in one of the nearby terraces in Edwardsville.

About fifty men of various occupations and grades were attached to, and drawing wages at, Quakers Yard. Towards the end of the Vale of Neath line's life it is doubtful whether ticket receipts covered the wages prepared each week by clerk Mr.Freddie Hake. Both stations were administered from High Level and a Leading Porter, Porter and Lad Porter on each shift under the supervision of the Station Master handled the stations' affairs. The clerk worked days regularly, and during his absence or at such times when he was away, it was the responsibility of the Leading Porter to issue tickets.

The busiest times during this period were early mornings and tea-time when pupils from Quakers Yard Grammar School crowded the platforms at Low Level.

Quakers Yard Tunnel

The tunnel, through which the Vale of Neath line passed from Quakers Yard into the Aberdare Valley, was known by a number of names. It was referred to at various times as Cefn Glas tunnel, Duffryn Isaf, and Quakers Yard West Tunnel. To railwaymen who worked in the area it was referred to as 'West Tunnel', after Quakers Yard West Tunnel Junction signal box.

West Tunnel was the bane of footplatemen, gangers and lampmen who were required in the course of their duties to pass through its single, unventilated bore. It was 703 yards in length and straight except for a slight curve at the Penrhiwceiber end. Clearance inside the tunnel was severely limited and the space between locomotive chimney and tunnel roof was no more than one foot.

When constructed, the tunnel could have been fifty yards shorter in length but allowance had to be made for the existence of the Glamorganshire Canal – which pre-dated the Vale of Neath line by 70 years – the cut of which passed over the tunnel's eastern portal. In fact the bed of the canal and the roof of the tunnel were separated by less than 20 feet. In later years the close proximity of the canal and the portal of the tunnel caused problems for enginemen, especially those on the first train on a Monday morning during the winter. By

those days there was no Sunday traffic on the Vale of Neath line, and this enabled javelin-like icicles to build up and hang from the tunnel roof – it was the first train on a Monday which came into contact with these vicious obstacles. Caution had to be exercised by the footplatemen as the engine collided with the icicles which, for a few brief moments, made the cab a rather dangerous place in which to be.

The interior of the tunnel was a mixture of brick and solid rock. Manholes, in which many a railwaymen took refuge, were liberally provided. On the down side, cut into solid rock and about half way through the tunnel, a platelayers' cabin was provided.

Tokenless single line working

The Vale of Neath line was double track for almost all of its length. There were only two single line sections. One was at Quakers Yard and was just over a mile in length. It commenced at High Level and included West Tunnel, double line being resumed at Quakers Yard West Tunnel Junction signal box. The other single line section was between Crumlin Junction and Crumlin (High Level) and included Crumlin Viaduct, though this section had originally been double and had been singled as late as 1928.

Unlike Crumlin, the single line section at Quakers Yard was tokenless and was worked by 'lock and block'. To explain how this system worked, let us imagine the passage of an up train from Aberdare to Pontypool Road. The West Tunnel signalman would have been warned of its approach by his counterpart at Cresselley Crossing signal box 'asking the road' on the block bell. The West Tunnel signalman would then send 'is line clear' on his instrument to Quakers Yard station box. If accepted, the block instruments would be switched to the 'line clear' position, electrically locking the down starting signal at the station box at 'danger' – this prevented a down train from entering the single line section and released the up starting signal at West Tunnel so that it could be lowered for the approaching up train to proceed. When the train arrived at West Tunnel, the signalman would send 'train entering section' to the station box. On passing the West Tunnel starting signal, the train passed over a treadle in the track. Once the train had passed the signal, it was returned to 'danger' by the West Tunnel signalman, and locked electrically by circuits activated by the treadle. On arriving at Quakers Yard station, the signalman would send 'train out of section' to West Tunnel box and the train ran over another treadle, electrically releasing the system for another train to pass in either direction, as required.

Linemen, signalmen and S&T personnel who worked at Quakers Yard often referred to a mysterious mercury cup

which was an integral part of the system of single line working through West Tunnel. A former S&T engineer who was responsible for the maintenance of the tokenless system explained the mystery of the mercury cup – it was fitted beneath the treadle and was the most reliable method of providing an electrical connection; the weight of a locomotive hit the treadle and this caused the mercury cup to tilt and it ensured the integrity of the system.

Quakers Yard West Tunnel Junction signal box stood in a lonely and damp location, on the up side, 14 chains from the yawning tunnel portal. The cast iron nameplate was almost as wide as the box itself. An up refuge siding was provided here and this was regularly used to tuck away an eastbound freight to allow a passenger to pass.

The gradient through the tunnel was 1 in 100 rising towards Quakers Yard. Heavy and lengthy eastbound freight trains required assistance through the tunnel. This was provided by the pilot, an Aberdare engine which, when not undertaking banking duties, spent the remainder of the day shunting the yard at Cresselley, Mountain Ash.

The banking engine did not couple up behind a freight train but gently buffered up on the move. It was not an uncommon sight to see a banking engine – usually a Pannier Tank – chasing its train in the vicinity of West Tunnel box. At High Level, the banking locomotive gradually dropped off the train, passing control of the load to

the train engine, but it was required to run beyond the station to a signal and crossover in readiness for the return to Cresselley.

The decline
It was mentioned earlier that the Joint Line Viaduct would eventually turn out to be the Achilles Heel of the Joint Line. Early one morning in 1951, a ganger, Mr.W.J.Rogers of Treharris, was carrying out his usual duties when he made an alarming discovery. He noticed that surface soil near the permanent way on the viaduct had become loose and this aroused his suspicions, which he immediately reported to his superiors. An inspection was carried out by the Divisional Engineer and, when a section of rail and ballast was removed, it revealed a crack a few inches wide running from one parapet to the other. Traffic was stopped immediately. An issue of the weekly *Merthyr Express* at the time reported that the crack, which ran diagonally, was 45 feet in length.

Thorough examination revealed that the viaduct – for many years supported by stout timbers – was in an unsafe condition and no longer suitable for traffic. As a result the passenger services on the Joint Line were withdrawn between Quakers Yard (High Level) and Merthyr as from Monday 5 February 1951. In the absence of Sunday services the last trains ran the previous Saturday, 3rd February. The goods services were also withdrawn between Quakers Yard and Aberfan. The unsteady state of the viaduct signalled the beginning of two decades of decline at Quakers Yard.

The rear of the Down (Cardiff) platform of the Low Level station; we are looking towards Merthyr and the connecting line from the Vale of Neath line is in the foreground. This picture was taken on 15 July 1959. *Photograph: H.C.Casserley*

Public passenger trains (i.e. excluding workmen's and any other unadvertised trains) at Quakers Yard High Level and Low Levels Stations, 4.00pm to 7.45pm on Mondays-Fridays

a) October 1947

Scheduled departure time from Quaker's Yard (p.m.)	High Level or Low Level	From	To
4.02	L.L.	Cardiff (Bute Road)	Merthyr
4.02	L.L.	Merthyr	Cardiff (Bute Road)
4.07	H.L.	Aberdare (High Level)	Pontypool Road
4.08	H.L.	Cardiff (Queen Street)	Merthyr via Joint Line
4.40	H.L.	Merthyr via Joint Line	Ystrad Mynach
4.50	H.L.	Pontypool Road	Aberdare (High Level)
4.56	L.L.	Cardiff (General)	Merthyr
5.04	H.L.	Swansea	Pontypool Road
5.05	L.L.	Merthyr	Cardiff (General)
5.38	H.L.	Pontypool Road	Aberdare (High Level)
5.53	L.L.	Merthyr	Cardiff (General)
5.55	H.L.	Cardiff (Queen Street)	Merthyr via Joint Line
5.59	L.L.	Pontypridd	Merthyr
6.33	L.L.	Cardiff (Bute Road)	Merthyr
6.48	L.L.	Merthyr	Abercynon
7.05	H.L.	Merthyr via Joint Line	Quakers Yard (terminates)
7.10	H.L.	Swansea	Pontypool Road
7.12	H.L.	Pontypool Road	Neath (General)
7.15	H.L.	Quakers Yard	Merthyr via Joint Line
7.40	L.L.	Abercynon	Merthyr
7.43	L.L.	Merthyr	Cardiff (General)

b) June 1955

Scheduled departure time from Quaker's Yard (p.m.)	High Level or Low Level	From	To
4.06	H.L.	Aberdare (High Level)	Pontypool Road
4.07	H.L.	Cardiff (Queen Street) via Nelson & Llancaiach	Quakers Yard (terminates)
4.19	L.L.	Merthyr	Barry Island
4.23	L.L.	Barry Island	Merthyr
4.35	L.L.	Quakers Yard	Merthyr
4.47	H.L.	Pontypool Road	Swansea
4.56	L.L.	Pontypridd	Merthyr
4.58	H.L.	Swansea	Pontypool Road
5.19	L.L.	Merthyr	Barry Island
5.36	H.L.	Neath (General)	Cardiff (Queen Street) via Nelson & Llancaiach
5.41	H.L.	Pontypool Road	Aberdare (High Level)
5.55	L.L.	Barry Island	Merthyr
5.59	L.L.	Merthyr	Pontypridd
6.14	H.L.	Cardiff (Queen Street)	Aberdare (High Level)
6.38	L.L.	Penarth	Merthyr
6.44	L.L.	Merthyr	Pontypridd
7.11	H.L.	Pontypool Road	Neath (General)
7.17	H.L.	Swansea	Pontypool Road
7.19	L.L.	Merthyr	Barry
7.23	L.L.	Barry Island	Merthyr

The remainder of the Joint Line was closed in stages, the last section – that between Joint Line Junction at Merthyr and Lucy Thomas Colliery at Abercanaid – closing on 9 May 1960.

At the immediate west end of High Level station, a little piece of the Joint Line did manage to survive. This was the junction and a length of the up and down track as far as the viaduct. Near the junction, a crossover was left *in situ* until the closure of the Vale of Neath line, though it saw little use except for the occasions when a crippled wagon was shunted out of harm's way, being used by shunting engines to cross from the down to the up line.

The closure of the Joint Line was no great loss to British Railways as its sudden demise occurred during a fuel crisis. Furthermore, it is doubtful whether the inhabitants of Aberfan, Abercanaid and Troedyrhiw would have suffered hardship at the loss of the line as it was more or less duplicated by the TVR main line. For those railway travellers in Aberfan, for example, who had used the Joint Line, Merthyr Vale station on the former TVR line was only ten minutes' walk away. However, passengers who had used the remote Pontygwaith Halt would have been faced with a greater inconvenience as the roundabout walk to Quakers Yard and Treharris was something of a nuisance.

The viaduct in its abandoned state stood for a further eighteen years. Although it no longer carried traffic, it proved a useful shortcut from one side of the Taff

valley to the other, providing the walker exercised extreme caution and avoided the gaping holes that grew larger and more numerous as the years passed.

Few photographs exist of motive power on the Joint Line during its final years. The reason for this is simple. The line's sudden closure came at a time when the small band of photographers who photographed the railways of South Wales extensively during the 1950s was not then fully active, and it took many of them by surprise.

Another thirteen years were to pass before the effects of the Beeching axe were felt. In the meantime, for those whose interests lie in the motive power that appeared on the ex-TV line at Quakers Yard, there was much to catch the eye. In 1953 the new BR Standard 2-6-2Ts began working the passenger service between Barry Island and Merthyr although they did not completely oust the ubiquitous 56XX 0-6-2Ts which had themselves taken over from various pre-grouping 0-6-2Ts. The big change came on 13 January 1958 when the Derby-built DMUs began to work the regular interval passenger services between Merthyr and Barry Island, albeit initially sharing duties with steam.

Meanwhile, at High Level, the passenger service continued very much as usual on the Vale of Neath line, the main feature of the line being the varied motive power which consisted of Panniers, Prairies, Moguls, 56XXs, BR Standard Tanks, Granges, 72XXs and on one occasion a couple of Castles on a Royal Train to Hirwaun.

The summer timetable for 1962 shows seven trains in each direction between Swansea, Neath or Aberdare (High Level) and Pontypool Road on Mondays-Fridays. The Quakers Yard branch, although not as busy as it was before the grouping, still handled coal in reasonable quantities from Merthyr Vale Colliery and some that had been hauled up the bank from Abercynon. However, on 11 April 1964 the last freight train traversed the Quakers Yard branch from East to Low Level Junction. Once the train had cleared the branch, East Junction signal box was switched out for the last time. As a through route, the Vale of Neath line saw its last trains on Saturday 13 June 1964.

Whereas DMUs had taken over the passenger workings to and from Merthyr in 1958, steam was still at work on freight, with the assistance of an Abercynon banker, until the end of 1964, at which time the English Electric Type 3 diesels (D67XXs – Class 37) took over all freight work. The diesels made easy work of Abercynon bank.

In 1969, two of Quakers Yard's outstanding landmarks – the Vale of Neath viaduct and the decrepit Joint Line (or Number Two) viaduct – were demolished. The event attracted a huge crowd of spectators. A colleague who witnessed the explosions recalled that the blast was so fierce that several windows in the adjacent Quakers Yard Truant School were shattered.

In 1971 the ex-TV main line from Abercynon to Merthyr was singled, with Black Lion, the junction for Merthyr Vale

The unprepossessing southbound platform and 'facilities' at High Level, July 1959. *Photograph: H.C.Casserley*

Looking out from the north-west end of High Level station, February 1961. The single-track line bearing to the left in the distance is the Vale of Neath line; the one curving around to the right is the old Joint line to Merthyr via Aberfan. *Photograph: Peter Barnfield*

Having just left Quakers Yard Low Level, a Merthyr-bound train, headed by a Standard Class 2 2-6-2T, threads its way along the Taff valley on 10 August 1955. The 'ridge' running from left to right in the mid-distance is the old Joint line to Merthyr – part of the viaduct near Quakers Yard station can just be discerned above the locomotive smoke. As a further aid to getting one's bearings, the photographer was standing almost alongside what was, at the time, the A470 (though since the building of the new A470, this section is now the A4054). *Photograph: Ian L.Wright*

The celebrated 'double viaducts' to the north-west of Quakers Yard were popular subjects for photographers, perhaps even more so when they were in their reinforced state. In this view looking north, a 2-6-0 is seen drifting across Vale of Neath viaduct towards the tunnel with a westbound goods on 6 March 1958. The abandoned Joint Line viaduct can be seen behind the train. The River Taff passes beneath both viaducts and to the right of the first arch of the front viaduct can be seen the course of the Merthyr Tramroad. *Photograph: S.Rickard/B.J.Miller Collection*

The Taff Vale Viaduct at Quakers Yard, photographed on 10 August 1955. This view, which looks towards Abercynon, shows the timber framework being removed. Note the two different architectural styles: that of the original Brunel single-line structure of 1841 is furthest from the camera. *Photograph: Ian L.Wright*

On 6 March 1958, Pannier Tank 6410 of Aberdare shed waits at High Level with the 11.19am Neath-Pontypool Road train. The abandoned cut of the Glamorganshire Canal can be seen on the slopes of Cefn Glas in the far background. *Photograph: S.Rickard/B.J.Miller Collection*

In this view taken from the signal box and looking south, 56XX 0-6-2T 5626 brings a train of wagons off the connecting line at Low Level Junction on 9 November 1963. The rear of High Level station buildings can be seen high up on the left. *Photograph: John White*

On 6 March 1958, a BR Standard 2-6-2T gets a Cardiff-Merthyr train of six non-corridor coaches away from Quakers Yard (Low Level). The train is a typical formation of the period on the ex-TVR main line. In the foreground can be seen the abandoned trackbed of the Joint Line which at this point swung sharply on to the Joint Line viaduct. Close inspection of the picture will show that rails are still in place on the viaduct even though at this time it had been out of use for seven years. To the right of the plume of steam is the locally infamous Quakers Yard Truant School. *Photograph: S.Rickard/B.J.Miller Collection*

We return to Low Level station for a final view looking north-west from the junction in November 1963. The two sidings to the right were taken out of use in 1964. The ex-Taff Vale main line to Merthyr is on the left and is being crossed by a Pontypool Road-Aberdare (High Level) train hauled by a 61XX 2-6-2T. In the final years of the passenger service two- or three-coach trains provided sufficient capacity on the Vale of Neath line. *Photograph: John White*

The basic 'modern railway' at Quakers Yard, looking south towards the Taff Vale viaduct in the early 1990s. This is what remains of Low Level station and the railway complex at Quakers Yard in general – just a single line and the Down platform with a small shelter. The private houses in the background stand on what was the connection between Low Level and East Junction. Note that the Up platform has been reclaimed by mother nature since being taken out of use in 1971. *Photograph: Author*

ERNE Photographs by C.Bergstrand; The Transport Treasury

The 3ft-gauge County Donegal Railways had four splendid 4-6-4 tank locos: No.9 *Eske*, No.10 *Owena*, No.11 *Erne* and No.12 *Mourne*. They were built by Nasmyth Wilson of Patricroft in 1904 to help out with the Donegal's increasing freight traffic. With 3ft 9in driving wheels, 15in x 21in cylinders, a boiler pressure of 160lb, weighing in at 44 tons 10 cwt and with a tractive effort of 14,280lbs, they were initially regarded as a disappointment, but after the fitting of superheaters they really came into their own.

Our four pictures show the extremely handsome, powerful-looking No.11 *Erne* shunting at Raphoe, on the Strabane-Letterkenny line, on 25 April 1957. We are left wondering why one of the largest 3ft gauge tank locos around had what must have been some of the smallest nameplates... *Erne* lasted until the very end of the Donegal, having claimed the status of the last surviving Baltic in Britain and Ireland. Her final duty was to haul the demolition train out to Letterkenny in the early 1960s (the line had closed in January 1960), after which she was laid up on the then-isolated sidings at Letterkenny. She was later purchased for preservation but, sadly, she was sold for scrap in 1967.

ON TOUR Photographs Paul Hocquard; The Transport Treasury

During the four days of the Easter weekend of 1965 – 16th-19th April – the Stephenson Locomotive Society and The Branch Line Society had their annual 'Scottish Rambler' rail tour. That year's tour started at Glasgow and took in the Edinburgh area, the Waverley Route, the Caledonian main line and Ayrshire. The motive power included an A4 Pacific, the preserved Highland 'Jones Goods' 103 and Caledonian single 123, and BR Standard Class 2 2-6-0 78046. For the section of the tour which took in the Balerno branch to the south of Edinburgh, it was 78046 which did the honours; our photographs show the train at Colinton, the first station along the branch from the Edinburgh end. One item of platform furniture appears to be an ancient coach or

van body. At the time of the tour 78046 was allocated to Bathgate – honest! It had been transferred from Hawick in January 1964; at that time Scottish sheds did not always change shed plates, and as evidenced here the repainting of the 'home shed' on the buffer beam after a transfer was also considered optional. The Balerno branch had lost its ordinary passenger services as far back as 1943, and the SLS/BLS tour train of 19 April 1965 was the very last passenger train to visit the branch. The branch closed completely in 1967 and the alignment now forms part of the Water of Leith Walkway which extends from Balerno to Leith and has been described as 'one of the finest riverside walks that any citizen could ask for'.

A cornucopia of gauges
The railway systems of Collier's Brick Works of Marks Te

by Ian P.Peaty

PRIVATE